Tim Booth is an intensive care paramedic who worked for six years in south-west Sydney, patching up the sickest, strangest and silliest of patients who called 000 for all manner of trauma and triviality. Prior to his career in healthcare, Tim was a motoring journalist who worked for *Top Gear Australia* magazine.

After deciding he no longer wanted a 9-to-5 office job, but still wanted to drive like The Stig, Tim switched the flashy Mercedes sports cars for Mercedes vans with flashing lights and left the media industry to study paramedicine. Honing his craft in the rough and demanding suburbs of Sydney's south-west, such as Bankstown, Liverpool and Campbelltown, Tim achieved the highest clinical level of paramedic – an intensive care paramedic – just three years into his career.

He continues to punish himself with the gruelling night shifts and long days that being a paramedic demands and occasionally revisits his former life in the form of freelance journalism on the side.

After surviving the worst that the COVID-19 pandemic threw at the ambulance service, Tim left south-west Sydney to pursue a (hopefully) more leisurely pace as a paramedic on the north coast of NSW.

YOU CALLED AN AMBULANCE FOR WHAT?

STRANGE, SERIOUS AND SILLY STORIES OF LIFE AS A PARAMEDIC.

TIM BOOTH

Pan Macmillan Australia

Pan Macmillan acknowledges the Traditional Custodians of country throughout Australia and their connections to lands, waters and communities. We pay our respect to Elders past and present and extend that respect to all Aboriginal and Torres Strait Islander peoples today. We honour more than sixty thousand years of storytelling, art and culture.

Some of the people in this book have had their names, location and other key identifying features changed to protect their identities.

First published 2023 in Macmillan by Pan Macmillan Australia Pty Ltd
1 Market Street, Sydney, New South Wales, Australia, 2000

A catalogue record for this book is available from the National Library of Australia

Typeset in 12.5/17 pt Fairfield LT Std by Midland Typesetters, Australia
Printed by IVE

We advise that the information contained in this book does not negate personal responsibility on the part of the reader for their own health and safety. It is recommended that individually tailored advice is sought from your healthcare or medical professional. The publishers and their respective employees, agents and authors, are not liable for injuries or damage occasioned to any person as a result of reading or following the information contained in this book.

The author and the publisher have made every effort to contact copyright holders for material used in this book. Any person or organisation that may have been overlooked should contact the publisher.

Aboriginal and Torres Strait Islander people should be aware that this book may contain images or names of people now deceased.

The paper in this book is FSC® certified. FSC® promotes environmentally responsible, socially beneficial and economically viable management of the world's forests.

For the food and alcohol delivery drivers.
You guys are the real heroes.

CONTENTS

Reality is almost always wrong.
– Dr Gregory House

YOU CALLED AN AMBULANCE *FOR WHAT?*

1

A CUT-THROAT BUSINESS

'A blocked nose! You called an ambulance for a blocked nose!' screams Big Phil, my partner and training officer.

It's my first night as a paramedic trainee and I'm in Macquarie Fields, the area of south-west Sydney I've been posted to in order to learn my craft for the next year. Already the words of an ambulance legend who gave us a motivational speech on the final day of paramedic school are echoing in my head. He'd just finished recounting the history of the ambulance service all the way back to the ambos who served in World Wars I and II, blokes who carried little more than water bottles and a few bandages. He described how they crawled through trenches and mud with machine-gun fire whizzing over their heads and flak raining down on them, providing care to soldiers losing blood and limbs just as quickly as the guns could be reloaded.

'But those days are long gone,' he said with an amused smile. 'Except if you get sent to Macquarie Fields.'

Most people in Australia have never visited south-west Sydney. Just hearing the names of some of its illustrious suburbs – Bankstown, Cabramatta, Liverpool and the aforementioned Macquarie Fields – on the six o'clock news is enough to make the most dedicated Aussie travellers steer clear for life*.

Gang violence, drug busts, horrific road trauma, welfare fraud, terror raids and assaults on emergency service workers are just some of the subjects you'll routinely hear when Peter Overton or Mark Ferguson spout the day's headlines.

The reason for so much drama is always put down to the fact that it's a working-class area. That's because Karl Marx never came up with a sub-category called the *not-working* class when he was preaching about how low-income earners do the grunt work that allows their masters to keep their riches. Clearly, Centrelink didn't exist in Marx's time. There was no welfare system either, and if you didn't work, you were too busy dying from Spanish flu or smallpox.

* The stories in this book might not help the south-west's reputation, but they're based on real experiences. Not to worry – ask any paramedic, whether they've worked in the Northern Beaches, the Shire or the bush, and they'll have just as many wild and bizarre stories. If I'd worked anywhere else I'd probably be giving that area a hard time too.

But not in modern times, and not in Sydney's south-west where, if you choose, you can still sit high up in the social hierarchy, all the while making the tax office think you're destitute. It's the only place in the world where you can have an AMG-Mercedes and a jetski parked in the driveway of your fortress, and still present a special card to your 'ambulance drivers' that states you claim welfare benefits and are entitled to unlimited, free ambulance visits.

I say 'visits' because these days one-way ambulance rides to hospital are obsolete. Often, we leave patients at home in the south-west. Around 90 per cent of our callouts are, in fact, deemed non-emergencies after the statisticians have processed the data from our case-sheets. Many patients never want to go to hospital in the first place. Some think paramedics carry a magic wand that we can wave over them to make all their maladies magically disappear. Others think by calling an ambulance they'll get a first-class, luxury ride to hospital where, upon arrival, a red carpet will be rolled out and a team of world-class doctors will be waiting to treat them, and only them, and that there couldn't possibly be anyone else in the emergency department with a more serious and acute health issue than theirs.

How disappointed most are when we explain the reality.

'No, sir, you won't be seen straightaway for the pain you've had in your lower back for the past six months. Yes, sir, you will probably go to the waiting room with about 50 other people and be at the bottom of the list.'

And yet it never deters them. Day in, day out, night shift after brutal night shift, citizens of Sydney's south-west continue to call 000 for non-acute, non-emergency issues that any reasonable person would never dream of bothering us for. I know this because I've lived it for more than six years, from when I was a trainee to my current role as an intensive care paramedic.

There are a couple of simple reasons this happens. The first is because you will be sent an ambulance for absolutely anything. Can't sleep? Check. Sore toe? Of course. Toothache? Sounds innocent enough, but it could actually be a stroke, so we'll come with lights and sirens because if the call-taker's flow chart gets it wrong or a language barrier results in the mis-triage of a real emergency, the potential for litigation is high.

The second reason relates to my earlier point about a certain special card. If you are the proud owner of the light-blue, rectangular piece of paramedic kryptonite that is an *Australian Government Department of Human Services Concession Card*, a.k.a. the dreaded 'pension card', then your emergency service is 100 per cent free. Not just once or twice, but as many times as takes your fancy in any given day, week, month or year. A service that would usually cost around $500, and thus deter the ordinary tax-paying citizen from ringing 000 for something trivial, can be used and abused for free. Zero consequences. The Boy Who Cried Wolf phenomenon isn't a concept in ambulance world.

But, I hear you ask, how do so many people, who live privileged lives on the surface, make it appear to the government that they require financial assistance? There are, in fact, many ways to do this.

Perhaps you officially work in 'construction', but only accept payment in the form of *caassh braahh* for the herbal and chemical remedies you supply on the side to high-flying finance types in the Eastern Suburbs. Or you've got a family connection to a GP who has diagnosed that your asthma, anxiety or pain from a car accident 15 years ago means you could never possibly be a productive member of the workforce ever again and must be put on permanent disability benefits. Then four family members will have to be your carers, so sign them up for the pension card, too. Or you're a single parent, despite the fact you and your husband still live together under the same roof in a perfectly harmonious relationship raising your children together. The government doesn't need to know, though, so long as you have a different surname from your partner then all is kosher. These aren't genuine pensioners I'm having a go at – they don't bother us – it's the kind of pensioner Tracy Grimshaw pursues on *A Current Affair.*

Of course, many genuine, hard-working people inhabit Sydney's south-west as well. This book isn't a vendetta against everyone who lives west of the M5 tunnel. And there are, of course, still genuine emergencies out here. The nature of the sprawling, high-speed motorways allow for some of the city's biggest road trauma, and the social predilections of those who live on the fringe result in some horrendous weapon-related violence. Furthermore, the ageing population and lower rates of health literacy mean complex medical conditions are in abundance in both the adult and paediatric population compared to areas of higher socio-economic standing.

These legitimate emergencies make for just as good a story. I've included a few of the best ones, but you've most likely seen all that on those fly-on-the-wall ambulance TV documentaries, which filter and censor said fly's vision of what our job is really like – no different to the editing techniques used on *Survivor* or *The Bachelorette*. What you'll find in this book is the real bread and butter of a paramedic's job. You will be shocked; you will be outraged; you will burst out laughing because of the absurdity. And you will utter the phrase which first pops into our heads whenever we arrive at someone's house: 'You called an ambulance for WHAT?'

Back in the 'war zone' of Macquarie Fields on my first night, I'm staring at a middle-aged, slightly overweight Indian bloke who's writhing around on his bed like an anaconda has his windpipe in a death grip, saying he can't breathe because of a blocked nose. I turn with a bewildered look to Big Phil and see my colleague's face has turned the same flaming red colour as our first-aid bag. Then he starts to yell.

Phil's an eight-year veteran of the job and has seen more than his fair share of timewasters. I'm just the latest in a long line of trainees he's been tasked with not letting kill any patients over the next nine weeks that make up my first ambulance roster. I'm guessing his frustration is from wanting legitimate emergencies to break me in. His nickname prefix isn't one of those ironic ones either, like when they call large guys *Tiny* – Big Phil stands 6'5" and is built with the 120kg of a rugby league front-rower.

The red shade eventually dissipates from his face and the Indian bloke's carry-on subsides into the retreat of a cowering dog – no doubt thanks to Phil's bellowing. Sensing my confusion at this odd reason for summoning an ambulance, Phil instructs me to take the patient's vital signs and then we'll discuss his options. With his oxygen levels at 100 per cent, his lungs sounding clear and everything else checking out normal, Phil tells the bloke to send his wife to the chemist to get some Nasonex – there's no need to take up a bed in the emergency department for a blocked nose. We head outside and get back into the ambulance to write up the paperwork.

It's a letdown, but ultimately an indication of what's to come over the course of my paramedic career: breakneck lights-and-sirens runs to callers saying they or one of their loved ones can't breathe, only to reveal they've been struck by a debilitating case of anxiety, cold, flu or, as in this case, a congested nasal passage. Having only just left the paramedic course at university a few months previously, I'm used to simulations of heart attacks, severe asthma, anaphylactic reactions and high-mechanism trauma. So my confusion at a grown man who never learned to breathe through his mouth when he has a cold is understandable to my mentor.

'Had to remind myself to dial it back a bit there,' says Phil, referring to his outburst at the patient. 'Don't want to get you a bung* on your first day.'

With the paperwork finished, we let our dispatcher know we're ready for the next case. It's a mental-health job which is colloquially (and a little callously) referred to as a 'psych'. The patient is a 20-year-old male who's threatening suicide. There's no mention by the caller of the patient being violent, having weapons or having committed any acts of self-harm yet, so it's been triaged as a priority 2 case. This means the job requires an ambulance response, but since the patient isn't in any immediate danger, we aren't to use lights and sirens to preserve public safety. I begin tapping the address into the ambulance's built-in GPS, but Phil just grunts a short snort of a laugh.

'No need for that, mate. I know where it is. That's my next-door neighbour's house,' says Phil. 'Went to him a few weeks ago too, tried to OD on that amyl nitrate shit.

* A bung is what we call a complaint against us. Sometimes it's because we took too long to get to the scene. Other times it's because of 'bill shock' – the phenomenon of horror that strikes a member of the public around six weeks after their ambulance visit when a large invoice arrives in the mail. These complaints never go anywhere because they're obviously not the fault of the paramedics. But the number-one reason for bungs – and the number-one reason for the hypertension of our managers – is because the patient will complain that the paramedics were rude to them.

Ended up in ICU for a few days. Sounds like he hasn't tried as hard today.'

We pull up outside the address in an outer Campbelltown suburb, where there's an elderly man standing on the front verandah arguing with two cops.

'Hopefully it's just a domestic and they don't need us – so I can pop next door and say goodnight to the kids,' Phil utters optimistically.

On approach, the argument is stemming from the older man not letting the police inside the house.

'I only wanted the ambulance, not police!' he's barking at them.

The cops are assuring the man that for our safety we won't be going inside without an escort, and we quickly agree.

'Mate, I know him, he's pulled knives out before, so the cops are coming in with us,' Phil says.

The man relents and we head through the front door. I turn right at the end of the entrance hallway, but my boot gets stuck and slowly peels back off the floor like I'm on the beer-stained dancefloor of a tacky nightclub on student night. It's not stale craft beer on my soles, though, it's a sticky crimson fluid trickling from the kitchen floor. The next discovery I make reveals Phil's 'pulled knives out' claim to be the understatement of the week. The walls of the kitchen I'm now standing in have been repurposed to resemble *Dexter*'s kill room, but there's no shrink wrap anywhere to be seen. The gyprock and various kitchen appliances look like they've been sprayed in a 360-degree pattern by a rotary sprinkler – if the hose was connected directly to a tank of blood.

'Doing some renovating?' quips Phil from behind me. 'Oh shiiit.'

His joking tone rapidly changes when he sees what's in front of us. A young man is slumped against the cupboard under the sink and isn't moving. His chalky complexion contrasts with the blood he's sprawled in like some disturbed human-sculptural interpretation of the Rising Sun Flag. The great vessels that pump blood around his body and give healthy skin its natural pink hue have been totally drained of their oxygen-carrying fuel and the man is a waxy, lifeless husk.

'I'll get the stretcher and another crew,' says Phil.

And then he's gone. Just like that I'm alone with the sickest patient in the world and it's only the second case of my so-far extremely short career. I'm frozen with incompetence when I hear a voice over my shoulder from one of the cops.

'What do you need me to do?' he says.

Completely forgetting the basics of paramedicine, or first aid, or even basic human functions, I hand the officer a thermometer and ask him to take the patient's temperature. It seems like a simple task and the only thing I can think of, despite the fact it will do absolutely nothing to save this man's life.

'How the fuck do I do that?' he asks.

I'm not sure if his confusion is from not knowing how to operate a tympanic thermometer (in which case he obviously hasn't got children) or from the idiotic task I've requested he perform on a trauma victim who's bleeding out. I tell him not to worry about it when a brainwave washes over me. Primary survey! D-R-A-B-C! The fundamental first assessment we're supposed to complete for every patient, the one they even teach first-aiders.

Okay, D for danger is taken care of since I've got the police with me, I think to myself. *Now to check for a response*.

I kneel beside the patient, reach out and give his shoulder a squeeze, and utter the classic 'Hello, can you hear me' in the most clichéd, uni-student-battling-through-a-practice-scenario way possible.

Now it's my turn for an *oh shiiit*.

The minor amount of pressure I've applied almost decapitates the patient. His head falls sideways onto his left shoulder, opening a fleshy crater on the right side of his neck that a human fist would easily fit into. It's now I realise my chosen career is going to be made up of a lot of *oh shiiit* moments.

I start feeling guilty – like I've played some part in this above-the-neck amputation attempt – when a blood-stained serrated kitchen knife I spot laying beside the patient gives me a moment of morbid relief.

I pick up on the fact that the patient isn't responding, or moving at all, and probably doesn't have a drop of blood left in his body. It suddenly feels appropriate to check for a pulse.

A smarter, more experienced paramedic would've just looked through the self-inflicted flesh tunnel slashed into the patient's neck and been able to see the direct pulsations of his carotid artery without having to feel for anything. At this point, however, I am neither smart nor experienced and am still feeling partly responsible for nearly beheading the patient. I reposition his head vertically atop his shoulders, as if trying to awkwardly mend a priceless broken vase that belongs to someone else before they notice the damage. In my situation, though, it's firstly to hide any more evidence of ineptitude from Phil, and secondly to feel for a carotid pulse on the left side of the neck where there is still some flesh present.

I press my middle and index finger up against the skin to feel for the distinctive throb of a pulse and . . . *oh shiiit* again. He's got one. It's faint, but somehow this bloke is still alive.

Phil could tell this as soon as he looked at the patient, which is why he went to grab the stretcher instead of just pronouncing him dead. It will take years of my own exposure before I gain the ability to assess how unwell a patient is within the first seconds of looking at them. But as I will come to learn, Phil was on the money this time, like most times, and it's at this moment that our stretcher comes wheeling through the hallway. I mentally exhale with relief that my mentor has returned as I remove the stethoscope from my ears, which I'd just started using to check the patient's blood pressure.

'He got one?' asks Phil.

'Nope.'

'Didn't think so.'

There's too much blood volume lost from the veins and arteries in this guy's body to generate a reading from the blood-pressure cuff. Phil dumps our carry sheet – a fold-up piece of tarp we use for picking up and carrying patients incapable of moving themselves – onto the floor and starts handing out large-sized gloves to the cops. Our backup hasn't arrived yet, so we'll need to improvise and use them for muscle to help lift the patient onto the stretcher and get him out to the van. We roll the sheet under the guy's limp body and two cops help us whip him up onto the bed.

We're halfway across the front lawn when an intensive care paramedic, Bruce, arrives. The intensive care paramedics are who we call when we're the ones who need help. They've got more training, medications and skills to use on the critically unwell. Bruce offers a glance at the patient before telling Phil to get in the ambulance and start driving. We're 20 minutes from the nearest major trauma hospital – Liverpool – and we can talk on the way as we keep treating the patient. Bruce helps me load the stretcher into the back as Phil hops in the front. He pulls out of the driveway and whacks the sirens on.

'Got a cannula*?' Bruce asks me.

---

* The small plastic tube we insert into a patient's veins to administer medications and fluid.

I shake my head.

Bruce has a quick scour of the patient's arms and shakes his head, too.

'Understandable,' he says.

Simple physics dictate that the more blood you lose, the less pronounced veins are on the surface of your skin – making placing an IV near-impossible in this case.

Bruce throws a large trauma pad at me and instructs me to hold it over the cavernous wound on the patient's neck, then commences his desperate search for venous access.

'Only two things we can do for this patient,' says Bruce, multitasking by treating and teaching at the same time. 'Stop the bleeding – which he's pretty much done himself by running out of blood – and get a cannula to try to replace some of his volume with IV fluids.'

'Well, three things actually,' he says on reflection. 'Diesel therapy. Step on it, Phil!'

'Copy,' Phil says from up front.

He pushes the truck to its limit in the north-bound lane of the Hume Highway. Ten minutes out, he reaches for the car radio and calls ahead to Liverpool Hospital's resuscitation section to let them know we're on our way with a critical patient. This gives them time to have the appropriate trauma team ready. I continue to hold pressure on the wound, Bruce's hunt for a vein is fruitless, and Phil pushes for the land speed record from Campbelltown to Liverpool.

We back into the resus bay at Liverpool Hospital and wheel the patient inside the building. Bruce gives a handover to the doctors and nurses – something I'll need to start doing soon, but right now my mind is still too overwhelmed to send voice signals to my mouth. The patient gets slid over to the hospital bed where a doctor is already waiting with a device that looks like a cross between a handgun and a power drill. He presses it into our patient's leg and squeezes the trigger, drilling a large bore needle directly into his tibia bone. The patient shows his first sign of life since we've been with him – a shriek that sounds like Steven Tyler getting his nuts caught in a vice. If he had any blood left to curdle, this scream could do it. More importantly, however, the patient now has a point of access for an urgent blood transfusion.

The patient's fate is now in the hands of the hospital's trauma surgeons. Over a cigarette, Phil recounts the job to several eagerly awaiting paramedics outside in the ambulance bay who heard the episode unfold over the radio. He also gives everyone a rundown of the social situation which led to this event, which he is somehow privy to.

'So the old guy is the sugar daddy and this young bloke is a rent boy he's picked up overseas and brought back with him. But the old fella hasn't got much life left in his *old fella*, if you know what I mean. So the young guy has been going out to meet other blokes his own age and cheating. But he feels guilty because the old guy has given him a better life than he had in the Philippines or wherever – hence the repeated suicide attempts.'

The bizarreness of the situation stuns me but does little more than elicit an amused grunt from the others before they walk away. It's the wildest experience of my life, but it's not even close to the strangest tale these experienced paramedics have been told.

And it won't be mine for long, either.

2

AMATEUR HOUR

'Get up! We've got a job!' shouts Phil from across the other side of our station's combined lounge room and kitchen.

The door bangs shut behind him as he heads towards our ambulance in the plant room. My eyelids are still peeling apart as my mind adjusts to the realisation that I'm at work in my new job. I didn't even hear the phone ring. Sleep-ins until the afternoon during university life don't prepare you well for the middle-of-the night interruptions of paramedic life.

We made it back to station after the chaos of the previous case, and the hangover from the adrenaline dump hit me hard: I passed out on the couch a few minutes into Phil sticking on a *Deadpool* DVD. These rude awakenings will take some getting used to.

I glance at my watch to check the time. Beneath a smear of blood obscuring the hour hand, it reads 1.20am. I scrub our last patient's unwelcome parting gift under the kitchen tap and shuffle out towards the ambulance.

'Someone's fallen out of a wheelchair,' says Phil.

He's fully alert and far more used to broken sleep than I am.

'Might want to grab a Red Bull too – you're picking this one up by yourself, fit young bloke like you,' he says, smirking.

I twist the data screen towards me and notice a line halfway down. *Pt is a double amputee,* it reads.

I'm standing in a bedroom in the housing commission area of Macquarie Fields with a 65-inch Aldi TV centred on the wall opposite the bed. It's being used to its full potential as a smart TV: a browser window fills the screen with the graphic cinematography of a clip from Pornhub's 'Homemade' section. An unkempt man with no legs lies at the feet of a wheelchair that's jammed between the bed and the far wall. The smell of body odour, empty beer bottles and years of cigarette smoke that's seeped into medium-density fibreboard fills the air. It's a smell I'll get used to in countless houses I attend in years to come. A smell you learn to accommodate but never fully block out. The smell of hope abandoned.

The patient, Jeff, is apologetic so I try not to show how grossed out I am by the situation and the stench. I also try not to think about what he was doing to make himself fall out of his wheelchair. He says this happens sometimes and he can't climb back into the chair from the floor by himself. Consequently, he also can't reach the TV remote parked on one of the wheelchair's armrests, so his evening entertainment remains on display for the unexpected guests we now find ourselves to be. As a sort of consolation, Jeff points out that he's managed to put on some underwear that he's grabbed from the bottom drawer of his bedside table.

I stretch my gloves as far up my wrists as they'll go and hook each of my arms under Jeff's from behind him. It's undignified for both of us, but there's no other option. I heave him up using the most bizarre deadlift technique ever witnessed by another human and plonk him back onto the seat of his chair.

'There's the money shot,' Phil says, beaming.

I'm not sure if he's referring to my unsettling heaving technique or what's just happened on Jeff's TV. I feel my arms tingle with a surprising burn, and I need to catch my breath.

'Jeez, how much do you weigh?' I blurt out awkwardly to Jeff.

'Seventy kegs, mate,' he replies.

'Fuck, I'm only 75 . . . and I've got both my legs,' I say between breaths.

I really need to work on my bedside manner.

'Pension card is on the living room table,' says Jeff. 'Thanks again, boys.'

'No worries, mate,' I say, hurriedly exiting his room and heading straight for the hand sanitiser back in the ambulance.

'Pretty heavy for a torso, wasn't he?' chortles Phil when we're back in the van. He starts driving off as I enter Jeff's details into our patient record computer from the passenger seat.

'Yeah, I nearly threw my bloody back out,' I reply. 'And sorry for my awkwardness. Got to start thinking before I speak.'

'Ah, don't worry about it. I'm sure he's been through much worse. Look what sinking all that piss has done to him.'

'What?'

'Made him bloody legless. Ahahahaha! Oh, and one more thing. You won't be 75 kilos for much longer. Especially not when you're done working with me.'

'I'll be fine. I'm in the gym every day and I don't really eat much junk.'

'Ambo arse* gets everyone, mate,' says Phil as he turns into a McDonald's driveway.

'*Welfare check for car 758*,' crackles a voice over the radio, indicating it's been 30 minutes since we arrived at Jeff's place.

---

* An international phenomenon that plagues the industry and consists of sudden weight gain, poor dietary choices and loss of motivation to exercise. Contributing factors include long shifts, broken sleeping patterns, irregular mealtimes and limited access to food options while at work.

'Halfway through a double quarter-pounder and just doing paperwork for a non-transport,' Phil says back into the radio.

'Don't let me interrupt your breakfast, but I've got another one lined up for you when you finish up there,' comes the reply.

'Looks like that's it for us tonight, then. Hope you weren't planning on getting any more sleep. Let's see what he's got for us,' Phil says, punching the non-transport button on the data screen.

'21 traumatic injury for you in Minto,' announces the dispatcher.

'Minooow,' whistles Phil, dropping the T and saying it like the breed of fish.

It won't be long before I start doing this too, mimicking the way most of the locals pronounce their suburb every time we get sent there.

Jan, 55, from Minto has all her own teeth, surprisingly, but still pronounces her suburb without glottalising the *T*. Her freshly painted house walls are a welcome contrast to Jeff's Essence of Winfield décor. I don't feel the need to put gloves on before turning the handle on her front door. Jan's complaint is an odd one, though.

'I got up to go to the bathroom and felt a twinge in my back,' she says, holding her left flank area. 'I must've turned awkwardly or something.'

'Okay,' I say, expecting her to continue.

She just stares blankly.

'Umm . . . so is it really painful?' I ask.

'It's a bit uncomfortable, yes.'

'So have you taken any pain relief?' Phil asks from behind me.

'Well, no, I didn't think it was that bad.'

'Wasn't bad enough to take Panadol or Nurofen for, but bad enough to call 000 at 3am? That doesn't make much sense,' he retorts.

'Well, I don't really like taking tablets anyway. I prefer natural remedies.'

'You don't like using medicine? You do understand what the *medic* part of *paramedic* means, don't you?'

'Well, I just thought I should get a check-up. Just to be safe.'

'A check-up? That's what GPs are for, not emergency services.'

'Well . . .'

Phil cuts her off, preventing us from spiralling any further into this vortex of excuses and folly.

'Look, do you want to go to hospital?'

'Hospital? Do you think it's that serious?'

'Jan, darling, I have no idea,' he says, sighing.

Phil bends down, offers a comforting touch of her knee, and adopts a softer, admission-of-defeat tone.

'I don't have an X-ray machine or CT scanner with me to tell what's going on inside your back. But if you want us to take you to hospital, because that's what we do, take people to hospital for emergencies, we can do that for you.'

'An emergency? Oh dear. Well, if you think it's that serious then yes, I think I better go with you. Will there be a wait?'

'There'll be a bit of a wait, there usually is. But waiting in Emergency is a good thing. It's when you get seen straightaway that you should be worried.'

Campbelltown ED's triage nurse rolls her eyes as I'm telling her Jan's problem.

'She taken any pain relief?' asks the nurse.

'No, sister. Didn't want any from us, either. Said it wasn't that bad.'

'Waiting room,' she grunts and walks off.

Phil escorts Jan to the double doors that separate the ambulance bay from said waiting room, and then opens them.

'All the best, Jan. Just so you know it's about an eight-hour wait to see a doctor,' he says to her as she faces around 50 people with varying levels of sickness, all packed onto plastic chairs.

'*EIGHT HOURS?*' Jan shrieks as Phil lets go of the door, and she vanishes behind it into ambulance history.

Phil's wiping down the stretcher when a voice comes through the portable radio on his hip.

'*758, just wondering how long before you can clear for a sick person, not alert, at Oran Park.*'

'Tell him five minutes,' Phil says.

He shoves the stretcher into the back of the ambulance and walks off, lighting a cigarette. Patients like Jeff are clearly no *memento mori* for Phil when it comes to his lifestyle choices.

My inexperience has me thinking there must be something genuine to someone who's 'not alert' at 4.30 in the morning. I hit the 'available' button, disobeying Phil, and the notes drop down.

A couple of minutes later, Phil slides back into the driver's seat and tilts the screen towards him.

'Nineteen-year-old female. Vomiting, not alert. What a bunch of bullshit. When did vomiting become a reason to call an ambulance?' he grunts. 'At least this will finish us off.'

We knock and announce the obligatory 'Ambulance!' to an already-open door and follow a strained 'In here!' down a hallway to a modern-looking bathroom at the end. For the second time tonight, my eyeballs cop a bleaching from a bloke without pants. This guy still has both his legs, though, and they're sticking straight out at a 90-degree angle from a toilet seat. His hands are pressed in a brace position either side of him on the seat. He's red, sweating and providing a soundtrack that sums up the night. I turn around and push past Phil to commence dry-retching from the smell.

'We here for you? I thought it was a 19-year-old female,' Phil says.

'She's in the upstairs bathroom,' he groans.

'So, what's going on?'

'Youngest kid came home crook from day care yesterday, now we've all gone down with it. We called Health Direct* and they said they were sending you guys.'

'Bloody Health Direct. Never call them for advice. Mate, you've all got gastro. But from the sounds you're making, the nurse on the phone probably thought someone was murdering the lot of you.'

At that moment, a pair of police constables enter through the front door. Then a pale and dishevelled-looking female wearing pyjamas, who's about 19, descends the staircase.

We're all crowded around the bathroom door in a semi-circle, all looking equally puzzled in a bizarre mix

---

* In the rare occurrence that somebody's trivial 000 call has miraculously not earned them an ambulance because our computer-aided triage system has not deemed them worthy, they are likely to be put through to a registered nurse working for a government health advice hotline called Health Direct. Now, I don't want to disparage anyone who works in healthcare, but honestly, if you're going to speak to someone over the phone who's dressed as a nurse, you may as well call one of those sex lines that charge $40 per minute. Only two things ever happen when a nurse is assessing a patient's health issue over the phone: either the patient cracks the shits that they're not good enough to get an ambulance and begins abusing the nurse (in which case the nurse redirects the call back to the ambulance service and they cave in and send the patient an ambulance), or the nurse will be concerned that the patient's symptoms may be serious. And since they can't assess them properly, *because they are talking on the phone*, they will request that the patient be sent an ambulance with a lights-and-sirens response. The most common call we get sent to that comes from Health Direct is the dreaded gastroenteritis.

of uniforms and disease – the world's weirdest Mexican stand-off. The guy gets off the toilet and starts walking towards us.

'Sorry to drag all you guys out here. I think it's been a big misunder–' the young guy cuts himself off.

His cheeks puff on both sides like a blowfish and he does a 180-degree turn. He lurches back over to the toilet and jams his head into the porcelain to unleash an emetic torrent. As he does, his pyjama bottoms slide down, giving us unfortunate spectators an unwanted stargaze at a brown moon.

'For god's sake,' says Phil.

One of the police officers, a young female around my age, with blank epaulettes signalling she's a probationer too, has a turn at running off to dry-retch.

'Look, you're all going to be fine,' says Phil. 'Sure, you'll still feel like crap for a couple more days, I won't lie, but you'll pull through. Trust me. Just make sure you stay hydrated. Small sips of water, not too much. Plain foods like toast and soup. Y'know, the stuff your mum taught you when you were kids. We'll check you both over quickly, then we'll leave you to it.'

I check blood pressures, pulse rates, oxygen levels, temperatures. Nothing out of the ordinary besides a mild fever for the male. I pack away our observation gear and carry the kit back to the ambulance. We exchange goodbyes with the cops and laugh off the absurdity of the situation.

'We'll do the paperwork on the way back to station,' says Phil when we're back in the car. 'No more jobs for us tonight, mate. That's enough for me.'

We pull in under the station's rising roller-door and I spot the day shift crew through bloodshot eyes. They're looking as fresh as scented wet wipes as they check over their vehicles. They greet me enthusiastically as the newbie. It's welcoming, but only makes my tired body feel even more broken. It's almost 7am.

'Well done, you survived your first shift,' says Phil. 'Go home, get some rest, see you next week. I'm going to hang around a bit longer and have a word with the boss.'

He opens the door of an ancient-looking fridge set against a wall in the plant room and twists the top off a Carlton Dry before heading into our station manager's office. I can't imagine drinking a beer right now. I feel like I've just had one of those all-night benders that's gone on too long, and the sight of the rising sun is further validation that it's time to stop drinking before more damage is done.

I get into my own car and head for home, eastbound on the M5 towards the city, sitting in bumper-to-bumper traffic as the early commuters of Sydney make their way to work. The glowing morning sun sits just below my visor and, via the headache it's amplifying, is the only thing keeping me awake. When I make it home, I crawl into bed without even showering because I'm so tired. I don't have to get up for work again tonight: we do two day shifts, two night shifts, then have five days off, but fortunately, my career has started on the second night shift of the roster, so I've only had to work one shift before my days off commence.

As I black-out into unconsciousness, I'm blissfully unaware of a first-shift souvenir the last patient has left me, one that's about to ruin my five-day break.

3

BURNING AT BOTH ENDS

I'm hurling chunks of oesophagus-searing vomit into my share-house toilet. Beads of sweat dripping from my nose add to the mounting effluence as I hunch over the bowl in a disturbed genuflection to a squalid tabernacle. Then my back end lets me know it's time for a turn. I do an about-face and almost slide off a toilet seat that's heavily lubricated with perspiration. I grip both sides of the rim for stability. The ensuing stench triggers my brain's already overloaded vomit centre and I need to make a split-second, high-pressure decision like I'm about to perform a life-saving procedure; do I want to clean emesis or excrement off the bathroom tiles?

I think of my housemates and opt to remain seated. Then in a bizarre twist of fate, as the spew arrives from the depths of my stomach, it propels directly onto a bath towel that's resting on its rail straight across from me.

Most of it manages to cling to the fibres, making my job of cleaning the floor easier, but still not giving me an easy future conversation with my housemate Paula, who owns the towel. I extend my gratitude to the god of household bleach and shuffle miserably back to my room to endure another three days of feverishly marinating through short-notice toilet skirmishes and a flash diet of Hydralyte.

'You touch your face when you're nervous, that's how you got it,' Phil explains when I arrive back at work three shades paler and eight kilograms lighter.

It's been five days since the end of the night shift that we worked together. Five days of the four-on/five-off roster that paramedics do. Paramedics who usually spend their downtime relaxing with hobbies like fishing or Bikram yoga, not – thanks to the gastro bug – brining in their own bodily filth from an inflamed digestive system. It's 6.30am and we're starting our first day shift, and Phil's got another scrap of unwritten paramedic lore to share before our first callout.

'Everyone in this job has a tic when they're stressed, you usually see it on the way to a big job, but you were going all night because it was your first shift. For some guys it's staying really quiet; others won't shut up. Some pick their nose; some burp a lot. I do this weird thing rolling my left shoulder around like a fast bowler warming up, which I can't move much because I'm stuck in the cabin of a van so it just looks like I've got Tourette's.'

I'm nodding in agreement when I realise I'm picking at an ingrown hair in my beard.

'Finish off checking the oxygen and medication kits for me and we'll go get coffee,' says Phil.

A Mercedes Sprinter ambulance runs on diesel; the paramedics who drive them run on coffee. Coffee is premium unleaded fuel for paramedics. Without a steaming takeaway cup of caffeinated angel nectar to start a shift, few paramedics will claim to be at the top of their game. Coffee gives focus, alertness, warmth and motivation. There is a small coterie of paramedics who abstain from coffee. But Phil assures me they also sit down to piss and cough when they fart.

Our shifts are 12 hours and 15 minutes long. Minimum. No one ever goes home on time. An hour or two of overtime is *de rigueur* when working in south-west Sydney. Most paramedics also get to work half an hour early to check the cars are properly stocked for the day. This is no quick task given the ever-expanding litany of equipment and medications we're now equipped with. Add to this up to an hour of travel time commuting between work and home each way and we're now looking at up to an 18-hour day. And only five or six hours' sleep to recover enough to do it all again the next day. You can see the need for more than a few double-shot flat whites throughout a shift.

We're sitting at a table outside a local coffee shop, chatting to a night crew whose shift is now over, when I notice an old guy taking photos of us with his phone.

'There a problem, mate?' says Jason, one of the night-shift paramedics, to the snapper across the tables.

'You've parked in a no-stopping zone,' he says, pointing to Jason's ambulance. 'You guys aren't above the law.'

I look over and see the octogenarian is right – looming over the candy-red ID number that's marked on the side panel of ambulance 755 is a matching candy-red road sign that indicates no one is to park there. It's the only spare spot left near the coffee shop for blocks, so I can see why Jason's taken it. He's buggered after a long night and just wants a caffeine hit to help him get home.

'ARE YOU FUCKING SERIOUS?' bellows Jason's voice from behind me. It's so loud in the dawn stillness, I come off my seat a little. Jason's on his feet and striding towards the man.

'I'll be sending this to the council,' the old guy informs Jason, holding a mobile phone threateningly towards him as if we're suddenly in a *Today Tonight* segment about dodgy tradies.

'We've just pulled a child who drowned out of a swimming pool and they couldn't be saved; DO YOU HAVE ANY IDEA WHAT THAT'S LIKE? Of course not. You probably worked behind a desk your whole life and got your meal breaks and got a decent night's sleep every night and never saw anything traumatic. Now you've got too much time on your hands and have nothing better to do than harass some ambos who just want a quick coffee and a chat with their mates after seeing the most horrific thing you could ever witness.'

Jason's face is aflame, and the volume of his voice makes other customers in the shop stare nervously into their lattes. The old man begins to capitulate as Jason's partner, Steve, wanders over and pulls him back like he's heeling a ravenous pit bull.

The old man offers up a nervous apology and offers to pay for all our coffees.

'Did you guys really just do a paediatric drowning?' I ask Jason as we leave the shop and head back to our respective ambulances.

'Of course not. But he doesn't know that. What if we had?'

Jason winks at me and heads over to his car with a smile on his face.

Twenty-year-old female having multiple seizures, reads the data terminal. Phil peels away from the kerb outside the coffee shop, the ambulance's sirens squawking and beacons illuminating the dewy morning suburban vista. He's in the captain's chair again because I've got to wait 10 shifts before I'm allowed to drive with lights and sirens. There's no traffic to dodge this early and I'm still shakily fiddling with my medication book to double check the correct dose of our anti-convulsant medication, Midazolam, when we arrive at the scene. Phil parks the wagon at the end of a Macquarie Fields cul-de-sac where fibro shacks haven't seen a lick of paint since they were built and Commodores litter the unmown nature strips of every second home. We're directed inside by a middle-aged bloke with a scratchy beard who's smoking a hand-rolled cigarette. He seems unalarmed. Inside, on the patchy, stained living-room carpet, a thin young girl in just a Pantera T-shirt and a pair of underwear lies on her back with her eyes closed. A male about the same age, who looks like the kind of bloke that has a car for his Facebook profile picture, is crouched next to her with a mobile phone on speaker. I can hear the 000 call-taker asking if that's the paramedics arriving. He replies that it is and suddenly the girl begins flinging her arms and legs up and down in rhythmic movements as her head lolls from side to side, unwashed brown hair flicking all over her face.

'Look, she's having another seizure,' says the frightened male.

I hurry to her side and begin unzipping the oxygen kit, ready to put a high-flow mask over her face to assist with her breathing during the convulsion.

'She's having a penis,' comes Phil's voice from behind me.

Both of us turn to look at Phil with shocked and confused expressions on our faces.

'A what?' we say in unrehearsed unison.

'A penis. P-N-E-S. A psychogenic non-epileptic seizure.'

'Oh right,' I reply as if I know exactly what Phil is talking about. 'Sooo . . . do I still put oxygen on her?'

Phil shakes his head and moves towards us and the patient. 'Let me guess. This is your missus and you guys just had an argument?' he says.

The man nods sheepishly. The woman continues jerking.

'And she doesn't have epilepsy or any form of seizure disorder, does she?'

He shakes his head. The woman's jerking slows.

'What's her name?'

'Alana.'

'Alana, open your eyes. Stop doing this.'

Her eyes don't open. The movements persist. Phil gives her shoulder a squeeze. Still nothing. Then he gently prods her eyelid. It flickers.

'I know it's raining outside, love, but it's not the shower I came down in,' Phil tells her. 'We're getting paid for the next eleven-and-a-half hours, so we'll stand here all day if we have to, until you stop this nonsense.'

Alana groggily opens her eyes. The jig is up.

'Now sit up for us and tell us what's wrong.'

She pushes off the palms of her hands and rests against the bottom of the couch without assistance. I check over Alana's vitals to rule out anything serious as she recounts the fight she just had with Dale over some questionable texts she found on his phone. The two have a teary make-up and we leave them to resolve their relationship dramas in the living room without the assistance of the emergency services. Another life saved.

'How did you know what was going on there?' I ask

Phil, amazement in my voice as we head back to the ambulance.

'Bit hard for them to simulate seizures on mannequins for you guys at uni I guess, isn't it? A person having a real seizure is unconscious, mate. They can't feel you flicking their eyelids, so they won't move when you do. Also, notice she hadn't bitten her tongue or pissed herself. Wasn't frothing at the mouth. Her movements were very controlled and rhythmic. Someone who's been having non-stop seizures for 15 minutes doesn't have skin that's as dry and pink as yours or mine, either. Fifteen minutes seizing is a bloody workout. They'll be pale and sweating like Jeffrey Epstein having his browser history read out in court.'

'But why would someone do that because of a fight with their partner?' I ask.

'Mate, if I knew that I'd be the world's greatest neuroscientist. But that's just the way things are in the south-west. Wait until they send you to Bankstown. People having pseudoseizures and pretending to be unconscious after fighting with their family will be every second job you attend.'

In a year's time his prescience will prove correct, but for now I must get through the rest of my first training roster at Macquarie Fields. From the start, Phil guides me through certain fundamentals of being a paramedic that can't be learned from a textbook. His tranquil demeanour leaves me in awe as we attend a broad spectrum of incidents on the emergency scale. We splint broken bones (usually cracked hips and busted shoulders) and titrate morphine doses to make patients comfortable without anaesthetising them. We retrieve trapped patients with potential spinal injuries from mangled T-bone car prangs. We pump drugs into middle-aged blokes who've had heart attacks (owing to bad lifestyle choices) so that their blood vessels stay open long enough to not die on us before we get them to hospital for surgery. Phil doesn't come close to cracking a sweat, while I continue to nervously fumble my way through.

Once I'm allowed to drive with the flashy bits going, I learn that Service NSW hand out Xanax with every driver's licence they issue. It's the only explanation for the ubiquitous vehicular morons who never notice the three-tonne reflective van nipping at their rear bumpers like a starved Belgian Malinois, high-beam headlights shining, barking *wiu-wiu* at a relentless 100-decibels. The two screeching paramedics inside the cabin seem to go unheard every time, too.

I rapidly become accustomed to the reality of the job as well. This is no child's *Fireman Sam* fantasy. There's no sitting around drinking tea on station, shooting the shit with colleagues until an air-raid tone rings out and we all slide down a pole, scramble to our trucks and rush out to save the day when 14 cars pile up or a natural disaster razes buildings to the ground and we're left to scour the wreckage for survivors. It's far from that.

Someone told me early on that you need to like old people to do this job, and they certainly make up a large percentage of our clientele. But no one mentioned how often young and middle-aged people confuse the idea of a sudden emergency with a minor annoyance. The man with the blocked nose begins to emerge as the rule, not the exception. People with minor chest and urinary tract infections complain to us that their antibiotics haven't fixed the problem – one tablet into a seven-day course of three tablets a day. Those with chronic back issues want a sudden silver bullet from us to rid them of the pain for good; they're not interested in going to a physio to solve the underlying issue. People who insist on caring for heavily demented relatives at home want us to tell them why they're falling over all the time or not eating their food and look at us with horror and disgust at the mention that they may need full-time care in a nursing home if they can no longer be managed at home. Modern society is used to having everything on demand; streaming services give instant access to every film and television show ever made, Uber Eats drops any cuisine at your front door in half an hour, and Amazon Prime will deliver any product to you the next day, so you don't have to converse with those other gross humans in shops. Ambulances have become the Netflix of healthcare.

We're supposed to be non-judgemental, but some complaints are so pathetic I find myself unloading my anger on Phil – who just absorbs it with his years of ambulance acumen. He's resigned himself to the fact that there's nothing that can be done from our end. As soon as someone mentions a word on the phone that sounds like it might be mildly serious, they get sent an ambulance and it's up to us to work out what they really need. A mild case of haemorrhoids becomes serious bleeding. Tingling fingers from anxiety become a stroke. Someone who mentions they have asthma is always having a severe asthma attack – when they just want their blood pressure checked for free. And it is for free. Every time. Because everyone produces a pension card that waives their bill – which is the only thing that would deter timewasters. As Phil is fond of saying, the truth won't set you free, it'll just piss you off.

The weeks of my first roster continue to be eaten up by people's minor inconveniences, and my frustrations continue to fester: partly due to the training opportunities I'm missing out on, partly from the existential crisis that has me questioning whether this is a sustainable career. But mostly because I'm mad that when we're stuck with someone who's been constipated for a few days and hasn't done anything to help themselves, the drowning child Jason brought up in the coffee shop could really be just down the road. And there's nothing we can do for them. Protocols prevent us from just abandoning the patient we're with for a potentially more serious one without completing a full assessment and proper documentation. And that takes time. Instead, another ambulance that's much further away will have to be assigned. And by the time they reach the kid whose lungs are full of water, it will be too late. This is the reason paramedics are sometimes grumpy.

*

We have a few false starts throughout the roster, but so far are yet to attend 'the big one' – a proper cardiac arrest. The false starts come in the form of callers saying someone isn't breathing, when in fact they've just been sleeping in their car; or a 102-year-old in a nursing home who's passed away in the middle of the night, but for some reason someone's decided that CPR might work on rigor mortis hours later.

Then it comes.

It's 4am on my final night-shift with Phil. My colleague is lighting up pitch-black neighbourhoods as we blast towards Ingleburn. He drives as if the call is legitimate, but there's an unspoken thought buzzing between us that we're in for another stitch-up. We're both also really tired. Outside the address, a teenager is waving frantically. He drags us up a staircase. I lug our defib and oxygen bag up the steps and Phil is right behind with the medication kit. Another ambulance arrives as we hit the top of the staircase – intensive care paramedics are always dispatched to every cardiac-arrest call as well as a general-duties ambulance. In a bedroom converted into a makeshift gym, a man of around 55 years lies next to an elliptical machine. Another teenager, the man's son and the other kid's brother, pumps furiously on his chest on the instruction of a 000 call-taker. He stands and backs away from doing compressions to let us help his father, but Phil and I insist he gets back to it. We're still putting our gloves on, and CPR can't be interrupted. And this man needs CPR. There's no spontaneous rise and fall of his chest, his lips are blue and when I kneel to feel for his pulse there isn't one. He's in cardiac arrest. I take over CPR from the teenager and Phil cuts off the man's shirt to apply defibrillator pads. Then Bruce, the intensive care paramedic, walks through the door, this time with his partner, Wendy, another ICP. They both immediately know what's happened.

'Why was he exercising at 4 in the morning?' Bruce asks the distraught family.

'He's just started a health kick and sometimes would come in here at strange hours,' the man's wife sobs.

'Are you guys Fijian-Indians by any chance?' asks Wendy.

'Yes, why?' the wife asks.

'He's had a big heart attack. Very common in Fijian-Indian men around this age. The sudden strenuous exercise has brought it on.'

Wendy continues to explain to the family what's happening. Their husband and father isn't breathing. He has no pulse. His heart has stopped. We're going to try to get it going again. We're giving him IV adrenaline to kickstart it. We're breathing for him through a tube Bruce has put in his throat so that his brain keeps getting oxygen. And we're doing CPR to keep blood pumping around his body and keep his organs alive. Well, I'm doing CPR. I'm the trainee, so CPR is my job until I collapse, while the others do the sexy stuff like put in tubes and give medications.

Ten minutes in and we haven't had a shockable rhythm, I'm sweating worse than when I had gastro, and Wendy is doing her best to explain to the family in layman's terms why we can't shock someone who's completely flatlining like they do on *Grey's Anatomy*. Phil sees I'm at the brink of exhaustion and offers to take over CPR. I catch my breath and get the next round of adrenaline ready. I push it into the IV cannula and during the next check of the man's heart rhythm see that it still hasn't made any difference. Phil shoves me back on CPR duty. He's already red in the face from two rounds of compressions as his years of indulgence catch up on him. We run the cardiac arrest to 20 minutes – the standard time before resuscitation is deemed futile if there is no cardiac output – and Bruce asks if everyone is comfortable stopping. We all nod in silent agreement as the family look on puzzled. They don't understand why we're stopping. It hasn't clicked that he will never take another breath, never speak to them again, never be at the table for another family dinner. Fifty-five years of life has just come to a sudden end at 4.30 on a quiet weekday morning in a makeshift gym in a suburban house. Four paramedics did as much as modern medicine allowed, but it was never going to work. There's a certain point where the heart has taken too much damage and even if the world's best cardiothoracic surgeon had been in the house, he wouldn't have made a difference. Bruce breaks the news to the family as easily as if he's ordering lunch. He's done this a thousand times. I'm glad to have him around because I've got no idea what to say.

'Not much you can, mate,' Bruce tells me as we pack up on the nature strip outside the house. 'Never say any of that "they're in a better place" bullshit or anything like that. Just tell them what you did, why you did it and that they've died. Don't try and make them feel better; you can't. Their family member has just died. They don't need some stranger in a uniform telling them everything is going to be alright – because it's not. It's up to them to deal with it in their own way now.'

A police car pulls up and Phil gives them a summary of what's happened while puffing away on another smoke. It's standard for police to attend any unexpected death just in case there's any foul play and to prepare things for the coroner. In this case, the autopsy will only show that the man had a standard heart attack.

It's close to 6am when we've finished cleaning, restocking our kits and giving all the details to the police.

'Surely that's it for us,' says Phil.

No sooner has Phil spoken than the dispatcher's voice crackles an apology through the radio; we've got a shortness-of-breath job a few blocks away. Phil drops his head defeatedly on the steering wheel but kicks over the ignition anyway.

We nose into the front porch area of a unit in a block of council-built flats.

Rodney tells us he's just woken up in a panic because he remembered he lost his credit card at the shops yesterday and is worried someone is draining his account. Behind me, I hear Phil walk out of the unit in disgust and let out a scream into the morning sky.

'He alright?' asks Rodney.

'Fine, mate, just been feeling a bit off.'

This bloke has no idea how serious the patient we just went to was compared to this ridiculous use of an emergency service, but how could he? And why should he care? We're free. And there's no one else out there who could need us more than him.

I tell Rodney not to panic and to wait until 9am to call his bank so they can sort it out for him. I assure him he won't have lost any money and that once he calms down, he won't feel short of breath anymore. I don't even check his vital signs or do any documentation – what's the point? He has a pension card, so entering his details into our electronic record system means he won't get a bill. And even if we 'forget' to enter his pension number and a bill gets sent out, it only means the slight inconvenience of a phone call or sending the bill back with the number written on it, and the fee will be waived.

'What a way to end the roster – with that fuckwit,' says Phil as he opens the beer fridge back at station.

He pulls out two stubbies and hands me one. This time I happily accept.

The incoming day-shift crew jokingly and customarily tell us we look like shit as we sip on the cold ones. Our eyes are black and baggy and bloodshot, and our hair is tousled. We stink of BO. We laugh about all the silly things we attended during the roster. Then, on a serious note, Phil tells me I did well on our bigger jobs and that he reckons I'll make a decent paramedic. This gives me more of a lump in the throat than any emergency ever will. We shake hands and I head for my car to drive home.

'Oh, one more thing before you go,' Phil calls from the other side of the car park. 'You're looking a little chunky.'

Nine weeks after my involuntary crash diet from the gastro bug, I've managed to stack the weight back on with change to spare. I'm down from six to two days a week in the gym because of the long day shifts and fatigue from the night shifts. Sugar cravings have been hitting every day. I'm now 85kg. Bloody Phil was right. Ambo arse is real.

4

HIGH STAKES

Caller statement: tomato stake in testicles reads the information on our data terminal.

'How the fuuu . . .'

My training officer Danielle lets out one of the most common phrases in the paramedic lexicon. As she scours the screen for more information, the possibilities run amok in my mind. Is this a bizarre gardening accident, like that which ended the career of one of Spinal Tap's numerous drummers? Some sort of sex game gone wrong? Has there been a melee at Bunnings?

None of these are the case, which I realise as soon as I look at the address we're heading to. It's a local primary school, and a nine-year-old has somehow turned his ball sack into a shish kebab.

I know we've arrived at the right place when Danielle groans from the driver's seat. It's a sight that makes every paramedic I know moan when they see it, including myself in the not-too-distant future. A bystander – in this case, a school staff member – is flagging us down by waving their arms frantically like they're an inflatable tube man at a car dealership on a particularly windy day. Whoever they are seems to think we're both blind and completely ignorant of the address information we've been given. It gets worse when she starts signalling parking instructions by flapping her arms as though we're two L-platers who have never parked a van before. Out of spite, Danielle parks in a completely different place than the one she's been signalled to.

We're led to the sick bay behind the front office. A young boy is splayed on a deckchair-bed thing that the school puts the unwell kids on. His eyes are closed and he's grimacing. Both his hands are shoved down the front of his pants, from which a disturbingly large bulge protrudes. It's just an icepack, thankfully, which he whips out before proceeding to pull down his daks. We're barely through the doorway.

'Jeez, most people start with hello,' says Danielle, heading back out of the room. 'You can sort this one out with him – man to man.'

Danielle is my second training officer after Big Phil. We're both about the same age – mid-20s – but Danielle hasn't known any other career besides being a paramedic. She got into the job straight out of high school and hasn't looked back. I took a few practice runs with other careers before deciding to become an ambo, so Danielle has five years of experience to draw on compared to my now two months. She's done a split-second eyeball of this patient, enough for her to know the situation isn't serious enough to require both of us. Her terse temperament sometimes comes across as callous or aloof, but this is deceptive as she can be deeply compassionate to those genuinely in need, after having a classic career-birthing epiphany when a family member needed an ambulance. Those with minor ailments don't get as much empathy. *Plus, burnout doesn't take long*, she tells me. Danielle's also savvy to the fact that a pubescent male with a genital injury would be intimidated by a tall blonde in uniform, so she's left the room for his comfort as well. Although judging by the speed with which young Billy whipped his duds down when we entered the room, shyness isn't a factor for him.

Just as I'm about to ask what's happened, Billy's dad bowls into the room. He's red in the face and panting. He has obviously left work at the speed of light and sprinted here from his car after the staff called to say Father's Day might now be out of the equation for his son.

'What's happened? Is he alright?' asks Billy's dad.

'We're just getting to that, haven't really had a chance to look yet. You almost beat us here,' I tell him. 'Right, let's have a look at the damage, young man.'

Billy peels the icepack away from his crotchal region. There's no sign of any part of a tomato stake. Instead, there's a tiny abrasion on the side of Billy's scrotum, and the cold of the icepack has already helped to clot off any active bleeding there may have been.

'Looks like grandkids are back on the agenda,' I tell Billy's father, whose breathing returns to a normal speed as the redness in his face fades.

'What the hell did you do?' Dad asks his son.

Billy explains that one of his mates kicked a footy onto the roof of the shed near the school's agriculture plot and he climbed up to get it. In getting down, he jumped off backwards without looking below. He landed exactly where the school's tomato vines were growing.

I give Billy a couple of Panadol and a sterile dressing to hold on the wound – to keep it clean and stop it bleeding any further – and then tell Dad to run Billy to the GP for a tetanus shot. All of which could have easily been arranged by the school but instead, due to various legal reasons that define the bubble-wrapped world in which schools must now preserve children, an emergency ambulance was called and a minor scratch was mistaken for a deadly impalement.

I head back out to the ambulance where Danielle is waiting and recount the story.

'Shit, he's lucky,' she says. 'That stake could've easily made him into one of those chipolata-on-a-stick hors d'oeuvres you see at weddings.'

And so goes my introduction to a lifetime of swinging from the noose of gallows humour.

*

We make a beeline for our station, with the aim of having a smoko break at a table instead of off the top of our eskies in the front seats of the ambulance. The nose of the truck peeks under the huge remote-controlled roller door that serves as the entry-exit point for our ambulances and keeps unsavoury types from entering the station and thieving restricted medications like Morphine and Fentanyl* that we have stored. At that moment, the dispatcher breaks the news that we'll be dining al fresco today; someone has some abdominal pain. It's a low-priority job but because it's been sitting in the queue for more than an hour, it supersedes our need to eat and rehydrate with dignity and hygiene.

Frustrated, Danielle snaps shut the lid of her lunchbox.

If they could talk, ambulance walls would recount a sordid history of vomiting, bleeding, births and, well, death. The chance of some unsavoury micro-organisms calling our workspace – and makeshift dining area – home is high, no matter how much isopropyl alcohol is used. But despite how unappetising dining inside our mobile hyperbaric chamber of bacteria is, everyone must eat – hence why Danielle is reading the job notes through mouthfuls of mushed banana. I nudge the gear selector into reverse and the truck's warning beeps

* A synthetic opioid like morphine, except it's made in a lab instead of grown from a plant and is 100 times more potent. It's increasingly being cut into street heroin – the morbid theory being that the extra strength causes more unexpected ODs and deaths, so word gets around that whichever dealer sold it must have the 'good shit' because it's killing people.

echo through the empty station as we back out onto the street.

'Seventeen-year-old with abdominal pains,' groans Danielle, as flecks of spittle and banana string arc through the sunlight piercing our windscreen. 'Probably bloody period pain.'

I scan an ordinary street in Ingleburn for the right house number when Danielle lets out a sardonic grunt.

'It's the one over there with all the cars in the driveway. Haven't you learned that yet? It's always the house with the most cars out the front.'

It's impossible for me to reverse into the large driveway because it's occupied by a people mover, a ute and two hatchbacks, so I bring the van to rest against the curb.

'Don't ever buy a Toyota; they don't work,' says an irritated Danielle.

'Huh?'

'Look, they all drive Toyotas,' she says, pointing to the array of vehicles. 'And they're obviously all broken because no one was able to take her to the GP.'

Her demeanour changes instantly as she raps on the property's screen door and offers a cheerful, 'Hello! Ambulance!'

A large Islander kid answers the door. He looks about 14 but is already the size of two men.

'Hello, who are we here for?' chirps Danielle.

'My sister,' says the kid as he motions down a hallway to the kitchen.

Someone who looks like they could be the twin of the kid who answered the door is leaning against a kitchen bench. As we get closer, the figure is, in fact, a female, but no less imposing than her younger brother.

'What's your name, love?' asks Danielle.

'Nevaeh,' she replies in discomfort, one hand cupping her lower abdomen.

'Of course it is,' smiles Danielle. 'And what can we do for you today, Nevaeh?'

'This pain,' says Nevaeh. 'I've had it since last ni–'

Nevaeh stops suddenly. Her eyes freeze wide, and a ghostly pallor strikes her face. Then she makes a noise and motion that's somewhere between a burp and a dry retch. She arches her lower back, both palms pressing into her lumbar region, and lets out a scream. The outline of a bowling-ball sized lump falls from her pelvic region and slides down the right leg of her tracksuit pants. The lump gets caught at the bottom of the pants, between the elastic hem and the top of her right shoe.

Then the lump starts crying.

Danielle recoils. Her scream matches Nevaeh's. I just stand there, dumbstruck. I stare at Danielle. She stares back. Time unfreezes when Danielle instinctively unclips the trauma scissors from her belt and starts delicately snipping at the bottom of Nevaeh's pants. She cuts an upwards slit and a greyish-blue mucous-covered newborn baby emerges. Its umbilical cord makes it look like it's dangling from a bungee rope.

'Get me some towels!' Danielle yells at everyone and no one.

Nevaeh's brother returns with some fresh bath towels and Danielle rubs and dries the child with vigour. I watch as the moisture dissipates, and the baby's colour morphs into a healthy pink. It continues to cry and squirm in Danielle's arms. Good signs, I recall from training. I'm still motionless with disbelief at what I've just witnessed.

'Umm, congratulations. It's a girl.'

Danielle awkwardly hands the baby to its mother.

'Thank you. I didn't even know I was pregnant.'

'What?'

'Yeah, I've been getting these strange back pains on and off the last few months, and my periods have just been spotty. But I didn't even think I could be pregnant again.'

Danielle shrugs.

'Better go get the maternity kit,' she tells me.

I stop feeling completely useless during yet another terrifying and bizarre medical anomaly and retreat to the ambulance. I return with a kit containing sterile scissors, umbilical cord clamps, baby clothes and wraps.

'I'm guessing Dad's not around to cut the cord, then?' offers Danielle in a gently humorous tone, trying to break the ice with a dark joke.

'No. Can I do it myself?'

Nevaeh begins hacking at a section of the cord between the two clamps we've placed to stop blood spraying everywhere when she gets through. She's chopping violently like an amateur gardener trying hairdressing for a change. Danielle stops her and guides her through one well-placed, slow stroke which severs the cord cleanly. She wraps the little girl in a swaddle and Nevaeh begins to breastfeed. Shortly after we deliver the placenta, Danielle gets me to put it in a clear medication bag for transport to the hospital. I try my best to make it look like I know what I'm doing, but handling the fleshy, gelatinous orb is another mental first dab on the board of Ambulance Bingo. I'm just relieved that I manage to get it into the bag before I drop it on the floor in front of a new mum.

'Thought of a name?' asks Danielle sarcastically. 'I think Danielle suits her better than Tim. Anyway, let's head off to hospital.'

'Just please don't let them ring my mum,' says Nevaeh. 'She still thinks I'm a virgin.'

'That was incredible how calm you stayed,' I say to Danielle as we're tidying up outside the hospital after dropping Nevaeh off to the birthing unit. 'A fucking baby just came out of nowhere!'

'Mate, I was bricking it internally. Certainly wasn't mentally prepared to be handling a cyanotic* newborn birthed from a tracksuit pant. Anyway, I knew it'd all be fine. God was on our side.'

'What do you mean?'

* Blue in colour, suggesting a lack of oxygen and blood flow.

'Nevaeh. You didn't think that name was a bit unusual?'

'I thought it was a bit weird and bogan.'

'You're right about the bogan part. It's *Heaven* spelt backwards.'

'Maybe we just witnessed the second ever immaculate conception.'

'Nope. We just witnessed another day in south-west Sydney.'

5

CRASH AND BURN

The dash reads 44 degrees Celsius. The truck's air-con feels like it's got the strength of an emphysema patient's tar-doused lungs wheezing at our faces from the other side of a warehouse. Danielle's stripped down to the T-shirt under her uniform and I'm complaining about us not being able to wear shorts to work like our Queensland Ambulance colleagues can. The sweat dripping down the back of my neck feels like it's cerebrospinal fluid seeping directly out of my vertebrae. It's a Sunday afternoon and we're both imagining how much better it would be at the beach right now, instead of stuck inside a hot van with a cooling system that's doing little more than pump the germs it's filled with directly into our respiratory tracts.

We make plans to head for the nearest 7-Eleven to get Slurpees and ice-creams to cool us down. But the

Ambulance Gods do what they do best, and before we can make it to the cold salvation of a servo freezer, our dispatcher tells us we've got an urgent job: a 1C chest pain.

Now let me digress for a minute.

The triage questions asked of patients when they (or their family or bystanders) dial 000 are the gold standard for prioritising ambulance dispatch. The gold standard, that is, if you ask the people who built our call-taking software, called ProQA. Ask any paramedic, however, and they'll tell you the questions are a joke. And the problems begin with the very first one.

'Emergency. Police, fire or ambulance?'

That's the first question you are asked.

Then once you've chosen us: 'Ambulance emergency, what suburb?'

And before both questions, a recorded message will have already played, stating: 'You have dialled emergency Triple Zero; your call is being connected.'

Three times. The word emergency has already been mentioned three times. This should trigger most people into thinking that there are others worse off than them and that they don't need to tie-up an emergency service for a headache or back sprain they've had for three months. Not in south-west Sydney.

The problems continue.

'Is the patient breathing normally?'

If the caller says no, even if they are calling for themselves as the patient, not only do they get the highest priority of ambulance dispatch (known as a 1A), but they are also sent the closest general-duties and intensive-care ambulances. Their call has trumped all others in the area, and they get two ambulances. This is essential if the patient is actually in cardiac arrest because this is the most time-critical of all emergencies, where seconds really can make all the difference. However, you don't need a medical degree to know that if someone is able to speak on a phone, they are indeed breathing and not in cardiac arrest. But our triage software knows better.

But let's imagine that the caller has said the patient is breathing. They will then be asked if the patient is conscious. Breathing but unconscious will triage as the second-highest category (1B) and also earn an intensive-care ambulance if there's one around. The problem here is that most people either don't know what consciousness is, don't know how to check for it or aren't willing to check for it. This category will often result in us being sent to people sleeping in their cars or on park benches, or drunk teenagers in gutters who couldn't handle their grog as well as their mates. The dreaded 'temporary, emotionally driven loss of consciousness' that is so commonplace in the south-west will also earn this category. Legitimate reasons that warrant the 1B category include drug overdoses (particularly heroin), traumatic head injuries, diabetic hypoglycaemia and severe strokes.

The last category of urgent, or 'lights and sirens', responses are known as a 1C. These are where the patient is conscious and breathing, but the symptoms they have stated are potentially life-threatening and mean we are still required to attended urgently. These include things like chest pain (in case the patient is having a heart attack), limb weakness (in case the patient is having a stroke), shortness of breath (because the patient could be having an asthma attack or allergic reaction) or severe bleeding.

Any 000 call not categorised as serious enough to require a priority 1 response will be given a priority 2. The highest category 2 is a 2I, or 2-Immediate, meaning the patient's condition is not life-threatening but the next available ambulance will be dispatched without lights and sirens and the job will not be held up to give crews things like meal breaks. A 2I might be something like an elderly person fallen, a mental-health crisis, a broken limb or a baby just born with no complications.

Lastly are 2As and 2Bs, which, in a very large number of cases, are jobs that shouldn't be sent an emergency service, but somehow still are. These are your back pains, abdominal pains (or *kebabdo* pains as they're known in the south-west), someone who has vomited once, cut fingers, stubbed toes, headaches, nightmares and all the other many trivialities people call us for. These jobs can sometimes sit in the queue for five, six, seven hours when we are busy – proving they are not emergencies.

Back to the present and we're on our way to a chest pain on the hottest day of summer so far. Danielle calls out the address and then taps the screen of the MDT (mobile data terminal) to get to the next page to reveal further information. We're heading to a 25-year-old male who is . . . sunburnt. He's obviously sun-scorched and peeling like a blistered baboon's arse. It's slipped through the cracks as a chest pain because one of the areas burnt must be his chest, so when the call-taker has asked if he has chest pain, of course he's answered yes.

We park the ambulance at the curb of his front yard and head across the lawn to the front door.

'Yes. It's open!' yells a voice from inside.

We make our way into a modern-looking lounge room via the vestibule inside the door, where a tall, muscular man is pacing back and forth, scratching himself furiously all over. He's wearing only a pair of Tradie underwear and the searing chilli tone of his exposed flesh is reverberating off the living room's white walls in the afternoon light, giving the room a pinkish hue. Every part of his body is ablaze except two circles around his eyes and two neatly squared-off blocks between the top of his knees and bottom of his Y-front legs. Both a pension and Medicare card lay in wait on a coffee table in the middle of the room.

'Spend too long in the tanning bed, champ?' Danielle muses.

'Fuuuck it's so painful. Just give me something for the pain,' the human lobster says.

'What's your name, mate?' asks Danielle.

'Jamal. It's Jamal. Look, I'm in so much pain. I just need some pain relief.'

'You need to invest in Banana Boat firstly. Then you should probably hop in the shower to cool that skin down.'

'I tried and that makes it hurt even more. Isn't there something you can give me? What about that green whistle thing?'

'Green whistle's good for broken legs and shoulder dislocations, buddy. Plus, it'll just make you feel drunk for half an hour until it runs out. Then you'll be right back where you started. You're going to be like this for days, so the only treatment is to keep trying to cool the skin.'

'I've . . . I've got a bunch of Greek yoghurt in the fridge. Would that help?'

'Don't be ridic–' I start to say.

'Yes. Yes absolutely.' Danielle cuts me off. She stifles a smile. Jamal is already in the kitchen.

He returns with the bails of two 2kg buckets of Greek yoghurt swinging from each hand.

'Right, what do I do now?'

'Put it on the burnt bits.'

So he does. Jamal slaps great handfuls of viscous, white fermented milk all over his body. He lathers it into his arms and torso like it's shower soap. He lets out groans of uncomfortable sounding relief. At least we know it's working.

'Keep going. Get your legs as well.'

Danielle is loving this and can't help but encourage it.

Jamal smothers his legs and then looks up curiously.

'Can you . . . can you do my back?' he asks, holding out one of the tubs to Danielle.

She looks blankly at Jamal, then at me, then back at Jamal. Then the blank look becomes horror.

'Oh, get fucked,' she says, more to the universe than to Jamal directly.

'I've done some shit I never thought I would in this job, but that's going way too far for me. You're on your own now, buddy. Drink plenty of water and take Panadol or Nurofen every four hours. See ya, pal.'

And with that we leave Jamal standing alone in his living room in his underwear, caked head to toe in yoghurt, looking like the world's worst Halloween snowman.

We drive towards the hospital. It's the nearest place with a toilet we can access, and we're needing it frequently today with the amount of water we're drinking to replace what we're losing in sweat. We enter the roundabout that precedes the hospital's driveway but swing all the way back around because we're given another urgent job. A teenage girl has chest pains and can't breathe at a sports field just a couple of blocks away – 500 metres according to the GPS.

We don't rush because the call-taker will barely be off the phone by the time we arrive. On our left are the unmistakable green fields and cheering sounds of a weekend sport facility. We glide along, scouting for an entrance when a note flashes on the screen: *caller says ambulance has driven past.* Somewhere buried between all the people movers and mini-SUVs there must have been a parting for us to drive into that we missed.

'Want to tell them to just drive themselves to the hospital?' Danielle asks into the radio. 'They're literally across the road and it's going to take us a couple of minutes to turn around in this weekend traffic. Looks like there's 400 netball families trying to leave all at once.'

The dispatcher doesn't answer. We both know they're not allowed to make sensible suggestions like that.

A car starts honking furiously behind me. I look in the side mirror and see headlights flashing as well.

'Are they seriously beeping a fucking ambulance . . . oh, I think it's the patient,' says Danielle as she pokes her head out her side window.

I find a spot to pull over and the car that's beeping and flashing tucks in behind us as well. Danielle gets out and strolls over. I follow behind.

'This must be serious. What's all the noise about?' Danielle asks the family of four getting out of the car. Father, mother and two daughters. One daughter is slightly red in the face and out of breath, but not in any great distress.

'She has pain in her chest and can't breathe,' says yet another flustered father.

'Her breathing is fine, my friend. She'd be in a much worse way if she couldn't breathe. Show me where this pain in your chest is, love,' Danielle says to the teenage girl.

She points to the left side of her abdomen, near her lower ribs.

'Umm, I'm not great with anatomy, but your chest should be up here last time I checked, darling,' says Danielle, pointing 15 centimetres higher. 'What were you doing when this pain and shortness of breath started?'

'She was running laps for athletics,' the dad interrupts.

'What? Running laps? Wait . . . so she has a stitch?'

'A what?'

'A stitch. Mate . . .'

Danielle gives herself a moment to take a breath and absorb what she's hearing.

'You've not only just called an ambulance from across the road from a hospital, for your daughter who has a stitch, you then proceeded to chase the ambulance down the road and nearly cause an accident. On a day like this when there's a thousand kids around the road.'

'So, you don't think she needs to go to the hospital?'

'I'm not stopping her going there, mate,' says Danielle. 'But I won't be taking her. If you need directions, it's right over there.'

She points to the visible top parts of the hospital building.

'Just be careful. It's so close, if someone hits a cricket ball too far from here it might hit you in the head when you get there.'

Later, when Danielle comes out of the hospital bathroom, she sees the girl and her family in the waiting room. They look anxious because no one's rushing to help them. She shakes her head.

'Let's go get the next one,' she says to me. 'In this heat, there's always going to be a next one.'

Far too often in our line of work, we're met with gruesome images and unsightly vistas when arriving at a scene.

I'm rapidly learning this with every shift of my probationary year.

For me, though, the mangled limbs and decomposing carcasses are always trumped by one thing, which I'm about to get a rude introduction to: unnecessary male schlong. I can handle blood and gore, but there's just no need for overzealous blokes to whip out their appendages and get us to check out rashes or bumps before we have a chance to protest that it's not our area of expertise and can be sorted by their GP instead. Paramedics are as interest-free as a three-year deal on whitegoods at Harvey Norman when it comes to these kinds of problems. But it happens far more often than it should – and it's exactly what's staring me in the face when I enter the front door of Reece's house.

We lock eyes and freeze, but we're not here to draw weapons (even though one of us already has). There's no clothing below the level of his T-shirt, and there's a good reason Reece isn't wearing any pants: because he can't.

As much as the job notes are supposed to prepare me for what I'm going to face, one can never be truly ready. When I nervously move closer to ask how we can help, I see there's a metre-and-half-long wooden handle protruding from behind him. Attached to the end are the scraggly, fibrous remains of what was once a mop head. I can see that the world's most diabolical game of Pin the Tail on the Donkey has gone seriously wrong. When the caller statement on the ambulance's data terminal said, *I've got a mop lodged in my rectum*, we didn't expect it to be still in situ, swinging around with every movement like a Channel 9 cameraman's boom microphone chasing down a love rat.

'What the hell, mate! *Pull it out!*'

Danielle's voice pierces through the hallway from behind me. After the day we've had, she's already dropped the illusion of compassion. Reece's lips begin moving to offer a reply, but no sound comes out. I'm guessing he's in some sort of embarrassment-induced catatonia. Then I notice movement coming from lower down.

Thankfully, it's just his hands morphing into various shapes in front of his torso, and my gaze doesn't have to drift too far south. The imaginary cartoon lightbulb that lingers above my head for moments like this suddenly illuminates and I remember another note on our data terminal that mentioned the caller was using a text-to-speech device during his 000 call.

'Oh right, he's a mute,' I say to Danielle.

Reece points to me and nods like an enthusiastic puppy, then he makes the same hand motions again, but with a strained look on his face. The plot of the bizarre pantomime thickens.

'I'm guessing it's stuck . . .' I say.

More enthusiastic pointing and nodding follows.

'But how? It's a straight pole. Just yank it out,' says Danielle.

Reece turns towards the wall, and the lengthy, wooden, artificially inserted rudder behind him pitches and yaws. He starts throwing his hands in a looping motion towards a pair of coats hanging on the wall, like he's trying to put a basketball into a hoop.

'Oh no . . .' I say.

'What?'

'I think it's gone up so far that the little hook thing on the end that you hang it up with has gotten snagged.'

Reece nods again, this time with sadness and deflation. I sigh in sympathy.

'Alright, mate, let's get you to hospital. Looks like they'll have to surgically remove it. We'll tell them you tripped over and fell on it.'

I may still be a newbie, but I've seen enough medical TV shows to know that this is the go-to excuse for cavity installation enthusiasts.

'How are we getting him into the ambulance like that? There's no way he can sit down,' says Danielle.

'No, I guess not. And with that thing sailing around every time he moves, if we try to position him sideways, we'll end up smashing a window. That's not a conversation I'm interested in having with the boss.'

'Well, I didn't bring my drop-saw with me today, so you better radio for the fireys.'

And so, a short time later, a rescue truck arrives, and a group of amused-looking firefighters disembark and begin handing various cutting tools to a probationer of their own. The nervous trainee gets the honour of neatly sawing most of Reece's mop down to a stubby, transportable length. With a quick mechanical buzz and a soundless flinch from Reece, just over a metre length of wood clangs to the floor.

'Anyone need a new paint stirrer?' quips Danielle.

The group of firemen collectively winces at her offer, wish us the best and head back to the safety of their truck with a new tale to tell around the station. We follow them outside a short time later, but not before Danielle has reversed the ambulance as close to Reece's front door as possible to avoid the prowling eyes of ever-snoopy neighbours and maintain a modicum of dignity for the poor bloke. He waddles out of his house and through the side door of the ambulance, mop stump waving right to left like the tail of a French Bulldog with a tapeworm. He contorts into a sideways fetal curl on the stretcher, and we hasten for the hospital, giving them a heads up on the radio. It's a courtesy message to prepare them for the fact that Reece will need to be reviewed by a surgeon fairly urgently, before a wrong movement ends up piercing a vital internal organ, and also to bypass the congregation of paramedics and other patients at triage that would only add to the suffering of our voiceless patient.

'The heat's really bringing out the madness today. He was supposed to go out and buy an ice block, not turn himself into one,' comes the compulsory wisecrack from Danielle after we hand Reece over to the hospital staff. 'Pretty good introduction to blokes shoving weird things up their arse, though. You'll be seeing them from now until the end of your career. Now, what's next?'

*

The next one is a 55-year-old man, again with breathing problems and chest pain. But this time, it's at a nearby Hungry Jack's.

We switch driving roles and Danielle speeds there as I recount the many restaurant-based scenarios doled out ad nauseam in paramedic training – usually revolving around choking or anaphylaxis. Both of which are possibilities here. When we arrive, I'm trying to recall the treatment regime for dislodging foreign bodies from the upper airways and the adrenaline and IV fluid doses for severe allergic reactions. A couple of teenagers munching on chips and sundaes point inside as we meander through the outdoor dining area, kit bags in hand. In the heat, wearing heavy leather boots, long pants, a T-shirt and an overshirt, and with the weight of the kits, I'm sweating before I reach the sliding glass doors. This job is complicated enough without adding in dehydration and breathlessness. They used to send us home from school on days like this.

A middle-aged man and his wife who've been enjoying some Sunday afternoon saturated fats await in a booth inside. With no distress. Except hiccupping. Constant hiccupping coming from the man. He's got burning pain radiating up from his abdomen to the centre of his chest. He's just eaten a Double Whopper with jalapenos. Too quickly, we figure. His ECG and vital signs check out fine. We offer him the obligatory trip to hospital because any chest pain could be a heart attack, particularly at this guy's age, and we can't rule one out – only blood tests at hospital can do that. Danielle tells him all this but adds that this is more than likely a warm welcome to the world of reflux for the man. Time to start having a Nexium a day and opting for the salad instead of the burger.

'I think I'll just see my GP about it tomorrow,' he says.

'No worries. That's great because I've just heard on the radio there's a child not breathing and it's only a few streets away and we're probably the closest ambulance,' says Danielle.

'Oh dear, you better hurry,' says the man's wife.

We're already out the front door and heading to the ambulance.

The siren doesn't get switched off between the Hungry Jack's car park and the address we're given, which is just a few streets back from the main road the restaurant sits on. Nothing is costing Danielle an extra second as she hops up and down in the driver's seat, hitting the steering wheel and willing the van to move faster. Oxygen masks and rolls of bandage fly from the shelves in the back and get strewn across the stretcher and the floor as the ambulance leans hard on an outward camber through the corners we take. There's barely any time for us to discuss how we want to run this paediatric cardiac arrest – the most stressful job any paramedic can be called to. Other crews are piping up on the radio, offering to help. None of them are within ten minutes of us, so we'll be going it alone for a while. Even though it doesn't seem like much, ten minutes alone with a child with no heartbeat may as well be a week. We almost speed past the house we're looking for and Danielle puts her foot through the brake pedal so hard that if I'd unbuckled my seatbelt a second earlier, my head would be through the windscreen.

Then my head hits the windscreen . . .

I'm putting my gloves on, about to alight from the passenger side, when a dual-cab ute slams into the back of our ambulance. The impact throws my unrestrained body into the glass and I cop a blow to the temple right where a professional boxer would look to land a left hook. I'm spared a knockout blow thankfully and gather myself enough to open the sliding door of the ambulance and grab the defibrillator and paediatric resus kit. I stride across the front lawn of the address alone because Danielle's already at the back of the ambulance spraying so much malediction at the driver of the ute, she could be auditioning for a Tarantino film. It looks like I'm going to be figuring out this one solo to begin with. I'm halfway across the grass. The temperature has hit its mercurial summit for the day and I'm sailing on a sea of sweat. My pulse pumps out a death-metal blast beat. The front door is open and I'm inside. A sleepy infant is rubbing his eyes on a lounge. A woman I presume to be his mother emerges from a kitchen. She looks remarkably calm.

'Where am I going?' I ask her.

'Sorry?'

'Where is he? The kid. The one that's not breathing.'

'Oh, just here.'

She points to the boy on the lounge, who looks like he's just woken up from an afternoon nap.

'Why is there an ambulance here, Mum?' he asks.

Mum is busy on her iPhone.

'Oh wow, Dad crashed into your ambulance, mister,' he says, pointing out the front window.

'Wait, what is going on here?' I ask impatiently of the mother.

It's extraordinarily difficult to shift an over-adrenalised mind focused on resuscitating a child to a mellowed-out state of Zen that's needed when one parent of said child has written off your ambulance and the other one appears to be on TikTok.

'Here, look, he wasn't breathing.'

She hands me the phone. It's not a viral video from a fitness influencer, however, but a recording of the young boy, eyes closed, dozing supine on the couch, chest gently rising and falling, peaceful as the Dalai Lama on Valium.

'He's . . . sleeping,' I say.

'Wait, wait for it.'

I keep watching. The slumber continues. Then a swinish grunt resonates out of the boy's nose.

'There, right there. That noise. He stopped breathing. What was that noise? What do we do?'

Had this been 15 years earlier, I'd be expecting Ashton Kutcher and a camera crew to enter the room.

'He . . . he's snoring,' I offer.

A blank look.

'Snoring?'

Danielle bursts through the front door carrying our medication kit with an embarrassed but curious-looking man I now know to be the boy's father behind her. He spots his son and races over to embrace him.

'What happened?' he asks his wife, angst on his face.

'He stopped breathing while he was sleeping,' she tells him.

He looks panicked. Danielle is watching the video on the phone I've just handed to her.

'What the . . . he's snoring. You called an ambulance and said your kid wasn't breathing because he snored in his sleep?'

A classic Black Hawk helicopter parent who isn't aware children can snore.

Danielle hands the phone back to me and walks out the door. I return it to the still-bewildered mother. The father looks ropable. I'm not sure whether he's more furious at the fact that his wife has called an ambulance because his son was snoring, or because in doing so she caused him to rush home and destroy an ambulance in the process. I give him a defeated shrug and follow Danielle.

My colleague is standing on the nature strip with her hand on her hips, surveying the damage to the back of the ambulance.

'Better an ambulance being written off than a kid, I guess,' she says to me. 'I'll buy you a six-pack if you do the paperwork for this one. I'll need a beer after today anyway. It's way too hot and I fucking hate paperwork.'

6

CELL SERVICE

It's 1.43am and we've found ourselves at one of the many nursing homes that pepper the suburbs of Sydney's south-west. Great, monstrous, sprawling residential facilities with hallways reeking of talcum powder and urinary tract infections. Some are nicely renovated and feature timber panels, reproduction Monet paintings and unsoiled carpets. But most are worn-out, dormitory-style, brick-veneer labyrinths that hide society's forgotten generation behind each door: out-of-sight and out-of-mind elderly parents and grandparents considered too difficult or too burdensome to be cared for at home by their offspring. Regardless of décor level, the smell is the same in both types of facility, and we've found ourselves at one of the latter versions.

The registered nurse (RN) is flustered as she flips through our patient's paperwork in search of answers to the questions Terry is firing at her like a medical Gatling gun.

'What's her normal GCS*?'

'Is she on blood-thinners?'

'What's her advanced care plan?'

Terry has been in the job longer than I've been alive. He's forgotten more cases than I've attended. He's been to so many patients at this nursing home, he reckons they should name a wing after him. Retirement is looming for Terry, and it shows. On night shifts he's forever rubbing his eyes under the thick black frames of his glasses, and the few strands of grey hair left on his head are different from the presidential brown coiffure that once adorned his bonce in old photos I've seen around the station. Now he's more Hans Moleman than Hans Gruber.

Is this what 40 years of night shifts does to you? I wonder.

Terry is the last paramedic responsible for my training before I'm back in ambulance school for the brief course that precedes me becoming a fully qualified

* Glasgow Coma Scale – a measure of a patient's level of consciousness via a score from 3 (totally unconscious) to 15 (fully alert and responsive). Points are gained and lost by how the patient responds with their eyes, voice and movement to verbal or painful stimuli. For example, someone who has just had blunt-force trauma to their head may only open their eyes with a vigorous rub to the sternum, have confused speech and jerk their arms around, indicating a GCS of around 9 or 10, and that they are quite unwell. Someone who is in cardiac arrest is a GCS of 3 because they are dead and thus will not respond to any stimuli. The average nursing home patient is a GCS of 14 because, due to the prevalence of dementia, they normally only lose one point for confused speech. A common problem in the south-west is patients pretending to have a decreased GCS for various reasons.

paramedic – and then potentially being responsible for trainees of my own. Nothing fazes Terry anymore. Rushing stroke patients to hospital before their brains starve of oxygen is as routine as his morning shave. Delivering babies – in a lounge room, a passenger-seat footwell at the side of a major highway or on the steps of the ambulance before the patient manages to get on the stretcher – doesn't get his heart rate above 50 beats per minute (equally it could just be the beta blockers he's on). We continue to navigate these emergencies just as frequently as we do the absurd calls – like the lady who had blurry vision all day, which we resolved by pointing out that her glasses were sitting on top of her head. Or the man who couldn't get off the couch because he was so dizzy, which we deduced was due to him being severely dehydrated while his wife was away – and he had no idea how to cook or shop for himself. Everything is another rung on the ladder of confidence but the idea of being a fully qualified paramedic after only 10 months as a trainee is as daunting as running head-on at a pissed-off Sonny Bill Williams who's just found out there's no free bathroom stalls at the pub.

Tonight, we're here for Dorothy. She's gone for a late-night wander through the care-home corridors and had a tumble, as so many Alzheimer's sufferers are wont to do. It's an unwitnessed fall, which if you're playing Ambulance Bingo, is a guaranteed mark-off on each shift. Her forehead sports a brand-new egg and it's not of the Fabergé variety. Otherwise, she's in good spirits for a 97-year-old, and all her major bones look and feel intact beneath her tattered nightgown. She's avoided the dreaded NOF – a neck of femur fracture which is usually what is meant when someone refers to 'breaking their hip'. It's an injury that's immediately obvious to any health professional because one leg has suddenly become shorter than the other and is rotated either internally or externally. And at this age it means never walking again and a slow, painful shuffle off the mortal coil.

'Would you like a chocolate?' Dorothy asks me, offering a used hanky.

I politely decline and explain that we're going to take her to the hospital for a scan of her head. Her paperwork states she takes Plavix, an anticoagulant that drastically increases the risk of an intercranial bleed when an elderly person has taken a knock to the head.

We use a slide board to move Dorothy from her bed to our gurney.

'Weeeee,' she exclaims.

I'm not sure if she's having fun or letting us know what's going on in her incontinence pad.

'She's for full resuscitation,' the RN tells Terry.

'She is not,' comes his retort.

'The family would like CPR and everything possible done.'

'She's almost 100, love. No amount of CPR is going to do anything besides disintegrate what's left of her frail bones. There's no way I'm doing chest compressions and defibrillating this poor woman if her heart stops in the ambulance. We'll be bringing her straight back here to the comfort and dignity of her bed. Er . . . sorry to talk about you while you're in the room, Dorothy.'

'Is it far to the zoo?' she replies.

'But the family want . . .'

'Look, if her heart stops in the ambulance, I'll call them myself and tell them. I don't care that it's two in the morning. CPR doesn't save lives at this age, it just ruins deaths. God knows if someone does CPR on my 90-year-old mother, I'll beat them to death with a used colostomy bag. They should make bloody DNRs* mandatory before you're allowed into these places.'

It sounds harsh, but I can't help agreeing with Terry. It's a dilemma I'll continue to face throughout my career: families pleading for CPR to be done through some belief created by Hollywood shows like *ER* that violent chest compressions will bring their frail, elderly, palliated or terminally ill family members back to life. That somehow it will reverse a lifetime of ageing and disease and that their loved one will just wake up, walking and talking like the past 10 or 20 years never happened, despite them now being confined to a bed with a life-limiting illness. This doesn't just go away with CPR – we're just assaulting someone's corpse. And if someone like this isn't quite in cardiac arrest but it's imminent, transporting them to hospital just means dying scared and alone in a hospital bed in a corner somewhere, instead of

---

* Do-not-resuscitate order.

surrounded by family in the comfort of their own bed. But still so many families insist that everything be done when, in reality, doing nothing is doing everything.

We navigate the stretcher through the facility's narrow corridors back to the ambulance in order to get Dorothy to hospital.

'Poor bird, I was probably a bit hard on her back there,' says Terry, referring to the RN. 'She's probably the only qualified nurse on tonight for about 200 residents, she's as buggered as we are and she's desperately trying to remember what they taught her at some third-world university 10 years ago.'

He's right. It's hardly the fault of the staff. The bigwigs who own these facilities are cutting costs everywhere they can. Minimum numbers of staff on minimum pay working with minimum resources to get maximum residents in for maximum profits. And they can call an ambulance whenever they want, for whatever reason, without cost or consequence, because all their residents are, obviously, pensioners. Terry reckons some of the best nursing-home cases he's been to are a dementia patient who wouldn't eat their dinner, a dementia patient who cornered two nurses, threatening to hit them with shoes, and a dementia patient who wouldn't stop masturbating every time his favourite nurse came into his room.

'Ouch!' squawks Dorothy.

Terry hits a curb as he pulls out of the modest driveway that the nursing home seems to have built without allowing enough room for the extra girth of ambulances.

The van jerks violently from side to side and Dorothy's creaky frame gets an unpleasant nudge it wasn't expecting.

'Sorry, love. Looks like they cut costs on the driveway to squeeze an extra room in the place,' Terry yells back at us from the driver's seat.

Or his eyesight isn't what it used to be. *Either way, there should be a Royal Commission into this*, I think to myself.

Dorothy is most likely sliding headfirst into the CT scanner when we get our next job. It's at one of the local cop shops and the only information is that it's a low priority for a 'sick person'. The desk sergeant leads us down to the custody cells. Behind a transparent door, sitting on a bench that's just an extension of the wall, is a dishevelled middle-aged bloke with torn clothes and a busted lip. His name is Bob and last night he had some sort of domestic barney with his wife. We're not here to treat the wound, though.

'Need you to watch him take his blood pressure tablets,' grunts the custody officer.

'I'm sorry?' comes my stunned reply.

'Yeah, he forgot to take his tablets last night coz of the blue with his missus. So we sent one of the probies* back to his house to get them. But we can't let him take them without supervision by a medical professional, so it's either get you guys here or we drive him to the hospital.'

---

* Probationary constable.

'So you need to get an emergency ambulance to watch a completely healthy bloke take one blood pressure tablet, with a prescription label that has his name on it?'

'Yep, I don't make the rules. Plus, it could be bloody cyanide for all I know. I got no idea what the hell Ramipril is.'

I fight the urge to say: *If only everyone had access to a device that allows instantaneous searching of that kind of information.*

'No worries,' I say, sighing. 'Guess I wouldn't know what to do at a siege or an armed robbery, either. Saves wasting a hospital bed as well. Some system we got, hey?'

'Yeah, mate. Everything is scrutinised and politically correct and triple-safety checked these days because somewhere along the line someone fucked up.'

I watch Bob take a completely normal dose of his prescribed ACE inhibitor in an entirely amicable interaction that's nothing like the image of a tattooed, bellicose bikie that I had envisioned it would be when I learned we had a patient in the police cells. I'm thinking about the hours of sleep debt I could be repaying instead of attending to this pragmatically unnecessary callout when a thud from a cell across the room almost jolts me out of my uniform.

A man even scruffier than Bob is slumped against the Perspex. Then he starts clutching his chest. I rush over to help. Terry and the custody officer haven't flinched and are wearing unimpressed looks across their faces.

'That's just Leon; don't worry about him,' says the officer.

'But . . . but he might be having a heart attack*,' I say.

'Bit of *incarceritis*** again?' snorts Terry.

'Yep, off to corrective services in the morning after breaching his bail again. I'll never work out what they reckon doing this is going to achieve.'

'Oh look, now we're in full-blown *status dramaticus****.'

Leon's now twitching, spitting and moaning. Some of the spit makes it through the gaps in the cell door and I chalk up another practice round of the famous paramedic recoil that instinctively occurs when bodily fluids materialise without warning. I begin doing my best to start a proper assessment through the cell door, but Terry's having none of it. He approaches from behind and, after flicking my safety glasses from the top of my head to the bridge of my nose where I know they should

---

* Sidenote: a heart attack (or acute myocardial infarction) and a cardiac arrest are not the same thing despite the confusion the nightly news creates. A heart attack is when an artery in your heart gets blocked by a chunk of plaque, formed from the spawn of bacon and cigarettes, and starts to starve part of your heart muscle of oxygen. You're still alive and talking at this point, but if left untreated, you might not be, in which case you may find yourself in cardiac arrest. This is when your heart has stopped, and you are not breathing. If you reach this point, it is very unlikely that you will survive. This is the same as losing half your head in a motorbike accident or drowning. Even when you die of old age, this is still technically a cardiac arrest.

** Faking an illness while incarcerated to attain sympathy, in the false hope it will help you avoid jail.

*** A bastardisation of status epilepticus – a severe condition in which epileptic seizures last longer than five minutes or continue in multiple bouts without the patient recovering in between.

have been, promptly tells Leon to cut his shit. But even Terry's veteran paramedic status isn't enough to placate an equally veteran malingerer.

'Chest pain . . . chest pain,' Leon gasps as he writhes on the concrete.

'Bugger it; we'll just have to take him to hospital,' Terry concedes. 'If he says he's got chest pain, he's got chest pain. Our hands are tied just like yours are with Blood Pressure Bob over there.'

Leon is more than happy to walk out to the ambulance now that he's heard the good news. His ECG and vitals are completely normal, and he's only too pleased to have a convivial chat now he's got what he wants. He's extremely open about his criminal past on the way to hospital, forgetting he's supposedly having a heart attack. His stretchered arrival through the emergency department doors elicits a groan from a passing nurse (who's clearly familiar with Leon's shenanigans) when he offers a cheerful, *'Hello, sister!'*

There's 15 minutes left of the shift when we amble back into the station after being out all night. Again. Day shift are ready and waiting to go out early for us if any calls come in during this brief crossover period, so we're safe from any more of the punishment that the previous 12 hours has already delivered. Before I officially clock off, I decide to check my emails to kill time. Only one thing stands out in bold: an HR email labelled high importance. This is it. My permanent posting. I could be getting sent anywhere – Collarenebri or Coonamble, Broken Hill or Blacktown. It's well known that there's only two types of areas newly qualified paramedics are sent to – bumfuck nowhere or metropolitan cesspools (which are revolving doors for staff who only hang around until they can transfer to somewhere more desirable). I double click the message and immediately spot one word that makes me realise Big Phil was some kind of soothsayer.

I'm going to Bankstown.

7

IT'S A TRAP!

'Don't hit me, you prick!'

It's the first time I've ever sworn at a patient. To their face, anyway. Plenty of times there's been some choice words muttered under my breath when someone's been rude or aggressive. But this time it's directed at a beery Asian bloke who's taken a swing at me and connected with my right shoulder.

We've picked him up after being called to a car that's crashed into a 'give way' sign. The police officers who meet us say he was seen stumbling out of the vehicle and talking on the phone while smoking a cigarette after he ploughed into the metal pole. Now, after being breath-tested and blowing well over the legal limit, he's suddenly claiming to be 'unconscious'.

It's well past midnight and dead quiet, with only a few dim streetlights illuminating what would otherwise be a bustling shopping area during the day. Crunching over the broken bits of plastic headlight cover and shattered window glass littering the road, I wander past the gnarled front-end of a generic silver sedan. Just a few metres from the wreckage, the patient is slumped against a thin fence that separates the retail shops from the road: head down, eyes closed, his chin tucked into his sternum. He's clearly breathing and not making any snoring sounds, indicating he has voluntary control of all his faculties – otherwise he'd be obstructing his airway and grunting like a pig with sleep apnoea.

After a couple of firm shoulder squeezes and a lift of the patient's eyelids – which he quickly makes sure to drop back down – it's apparent he doesn't want to cooperate. With the help of the cops, we grab a limb each and fling him onto the stretcher.

Unconscious people don't have the capacity to refuse assessment in the healthcare setting, whether their comatose state is genuine or not, and our duty of care gives us implied consent to treat them. Being unable to comprehend the potential injuries you have sustained mean that you must be treated for your own good. We can't just leave someone lying on the street because they don't want to talk to us. The fact that this patient is faking doesn't really bother me for another reason, too. It means a quiet and easy cruise to the hospital in which to do the paperwork undisturbed.

That all changes once we're loaded in the ambulance and I begin taking the patient's blood pressure. The tight squeeze of the blood pressure cuff awakens something inside this dormant drunken beast and, as his eyes widen, a flurry of closed-fist haymakers come out of nowhere. His movements are slow, impeded by his imbibing, but some of them make contact, including a particularly nasty one to my shoulder. That's when I let out the words I'm about to regret.

Of all the swear words that have been dropped in my life, this is the most poorly timed of them all. As I grab the patient's windmilling right arm and toss him back down onto the stretcher, my partner Cameron pokes his head inside the side door.

'Careful, mate, there's a TV crew out here and the camera's pointed right inside at you,' he tells me.

Shit!

Thankfully, this time the expletives in my mind don't complete the journey to my mouth. I need to avoid further disaster. It's my first night as a qualified paramedic, and I'm already picturing myself in the CEO's office with a termination letter in front of me, news footage playing on his office TV showing a member of the most trusted profession calling his patient a prick.

I tell Cameron to close the door and send the cops over. The patient has acquiesced into the stiff foam of the stretcher, giving me a few seconds to figure out how I'm going to explain this to my immediate manager. I figure it's best to be upfront about my impending debut on *The Project*, and I leave Cameron and the police to keep an eye on our friend while I pre-empt the boss with a phone call.

I call Deb, duty manager for the evening, and break into a rant about how she may as well give me the sack now because, by this time tomorrow, every news outlet in the country will be running footage of a paramedic assaulting and swearing at a patient. Furthermore, it's footage that'll live forever on YouTube, so I've accepted the fact that I'll never work for any ambulance service in the world ever again. Breathless at the conclusion of my tirade, I let Deb have her say and she relishes the chance to laugh at my predicament.

'You dickhead,' she chuckles. 'If there's footage of that, then there's footage of you being assaulted by the patient. Go and give the cops a statement and we'll charge the bastard. And don't worry about the swearing; that'll be bleeped out. And anyway, I would've said much worse to him.'

Relief floods over me. Speaking to the cameraman at the scene, he assures me the patient comes across as the bad guy. Somehow in the commotion, I'd forgotten about the severity of assaulting emergency services workers. It's even a particularly hot issue in the media at this time, where harsher penalties are being introduced for the crime. Current affairs weren't at the forefront of my mind when I was being physically attacked, though.

We still take the patient to hospital, albeit with him in handcuffs and a police escort on-board. He's more compliant now, and once we've handed him over to the hospital's care, I give my police statement. I find out later via an email that the bloke was sentenced to 100 hours of community service. Though the damage to me was minimal, I can't help but wonder if the same penalty would have applied to someone who copped it a lot worse than I did.

Cameron and I laugh about the incident when we arrive at work for the start of our next day shift. Neither of us saw anything on the news during our days off, so we're relieved. We're also both still getting used to our new posting in Bankstown, an area where the choice of fast-food restaurants and kebab shops is as saturated as the fat dripping from the rotisseries and grills housed inside them. This is also part of the reason it's the suburb known for being the busiest in Sydney for paramedics. Health literacy is extremely poor around here, so complications from people regularly shovelling salt and sugar into their stomachs causes many forms of acute medical issues for a significant portion of the population. The area also has a reputation for crime and violence. It isn't exactly holiday-destination material, except maybe for people from Liverpool.

All of this means I'm shitting myself. Not only because I'm a freshly qualified paramedic but because Cameron is a trainee. Which is what I was a few weeks ago. Demand for new paramedics means a lot of trainees coming through. And there needs to be someone to train them, so there aren't many double pairings of qualified ambos working together. I just finished a 10-month stint as a trainee at Macquarie Fields, and Cameron has just changed careers after working in border security. He's been at this station for only a few months. He's also 10 years older than me, which makes it feel even stranger that I'm overseeing him. Between us, we have less than 18 months' experience. But we'll figure it out. We don't have a choice.

There's still so much I haven't seen or done as a paramedic. Ten months isn't a long time to learn everything about out-of-hospital care. And being a trainee one day and qualified the next doesn't give you any superpowers or extra knowledge; it just means you now wear a different coloured badge and epaulettes and bear the final responsibility for what happens to your patients. It doesn't matter if Cameron can't remember a medication dose or forgets how to treat a patient with a stab wound; it's my responsibility to remind him. And if I don't, or get overwhelmed, then we're in trouble. Well, the patient is first. Then we are. Then just I am. Coroners don't look too kindly on so-called qualified paramedics who don't know how to do their job.

There's no time for coffee at the start of shifts in Bankstown. We've no sooner finished signing on to the data terminal with our staff numbers and checking our ambulance has the correct equipment stocked when the dispatcher says he needs us straight away for a 'high-mechanism rollover, Code Nine*'.

---

* Code 9 means a person trapped, usually in a car, requiring a rescue service to assist with extricating them. A person may be trapped by confinement or compression.

This is terrifying.

I'd experienced my share of trauma at Macquarie Fields, but something that eluded my entire training period was a major motor-vehicle accident, or MVA. Given the time of morning, it's almost certainly going to be on the M5 motorway, the major thoroughfare funnelling south-west commuters into the city every working day. Images of burning wrecks and scattered bodies fill an un-caffeinated mind that's still adjusting to a new set of work days and a 5am wakeup. Word comes through the radio that an aeromedical team will be attending as well. This is a specialist unit consisting of a doctor and critical care paramedic that brings specialised skills and medications to the most critical trauma situations. Until they arrive, Cameron and I will be managing ourselves.

As we speed to the scene, Cameron asks where the hell I'm going. I'm confused by what he means until I glance at the data screen and realise I'm going entirely the wrong way. The incident isn't on the M5 at all, but the image I'd conjured in my mind had me heading there on autopilot. I whip the ambulance around in a 180 at the next intersection and make for the actual address. It's a street in Yagoona, so this won't be a high-speed highway smash. That's not to say serious prangs causing entrapment can't happen on suburban streets.

But not today, it seems. We pull up and nothing appears out of the ordinary in a neighbourhood that's mostly still asleep. The only cars on the road are parked against the gutter, under a layer of morning frost. Then an older woman beckons us over from behind a fence that separates the front and back yards of the house we've stopped in front of.

How the hell does a car crash happen in a backyard? I think.

As I ponder, the neighbourhood is treated to an unsolicited wake-up alarm from the bassy mechanical belch of a Q-siren, signalling the typically bombastic arrival of the fire service. Two rescue trucks roar up the street from behind us, LED lights blazing and dancing off the houses and street signs, making everything around glow in a hypnotising cacophony of red and blue. The trucks park parallel to us, and in doing so give only their occupants the necessary access to the patient's driveway, while blocking ours. It's another patented fire-service move that will inevitably delay stretcher access and slow getting the patient into the back of the ambulance.

The firefighters rush towards the waving lady and though a gate. Cameron and I follow with a lag because we don't rush. No matter what vacillations I may have over how serious a situation may be, I always remember never to run. Running causes your heart rate to rise, which leads to an acute reduction of fine motor skills and critical thinking. Plus, if you trip over then you become a patient. And you look like a tool.

We round the corner at the end of the house's side path and sight our rollover victim. Next to a mobility scooter. He's completely uninjured and the water fairies are already righting the scooter. It turns out one of the wheels of Arthur's electric shopping cart got 'trapped' in an unconformity in the ramp that grants him access from his house to the backyard. When Arthur tried to power out of being stuck, it caused the scooter to flip, or 'rollover', chucking him from his seat onto the soft lawn beside the ramp. He hadn't hurt himself, but it was just too awkward for his elderly wife to lift him off the ground. We help Arthur back into the seat of his scooter, and marvel once again at how our faultless phone triage system turns a mild inconvenience into a major calamity when certain words are mentioned by a flustered caller. Somehow rolling out of a scooter because of a trapped wheel became *person trapped in a high-speed rollover*.

Cameron is holding back tears of laughter when he gives a report into the radio, insisting we'll be able to cope without the assistance of the aeromedical team, who are still yet to arrive. The dispatcher is pleased with the news because he already has us lined up for our second job. Being trapped is the theme of the day, he tells us, however this time it's someone in a nearby park.

And this patient is trapped by a magpie.

Cameron acknowledges the job over the radio so every crew in the south-west can hear what we're heading to and have a giggle at our expense.

'Copy the 38-year-old male, in a park, Code Nine by magpie,' he says over the air.

'Should we wear our helmets for this one?' I ask Cameron.

'May as well, we've already pulled them out for the last job. Be a shame for them to go unused. Let's do goggles as well, just to be safe.'

We mosey the few blocks it takes to get to the park and dismount from the van with our multipurpose impact helmets and smoke goggles on. As ridiculous as this job sounds, we may as well escape un-pecked. Plus, it'll help convey to the patient the preposterousness of the situation that's resulted in him calling an ambulance to help escape this confrontational Corvidae.

We find Omar hiding behind a tree in a far corner of the park. He's given instructions to the 000 operator about where to find him and disappointingly it's 200 metres from the nearest section accessible by car. We're more annoyed at how far we're going to have to walk than the fact that we've been dispatched as an emergency ambulance to this case, instead of a council ranger. Or a vet.

We find the police waiting with Omar. Somehow, they've been dispatched as well. They're arguing with him that they can't just shoot the magpie as he seems to be insisting, and when they spy us they gain some additional ammunition for the scolding they're giving him about wasting emergency resources. Seeing our ridiculous helmets and goggles gives them a laugh, though.

We're all at a loss about what to do for this man, who's absolutely petrified of emerging from his deciduous protective shield. He's been on a morning walk and has been swooped by a magpie for the first time in his life. He's seen some recent media hysteria about fatal magpie attacks and is now paralysed beyond normal adult function. We offer to form a ring of safety around him on the condition that one of the cops keep an eye out. Not for the magpie. For any members of the public who might be filming this nonsensical farce on their phone cameras. Omar reluctantly accepts when we inform him the alternative is us all leaving and letting him figure it out for himself, and that we won't be coming back if he calls again.

The cops begin frog-marching Omar back towards the car park with the two of us paramedics flanking them when a woosh of air causes the junior cop to let go of Omar's left arm. The bird has been waiting patiently and has recognised it's time to strike. It's made a kamikaze dive-bomb from behind and we're all in the crosshairs. We're suddenly the stars of David Attenborough's worst documentary effort. Omar squeals like a P-plater whose father has just bought them a new car for their seventeenth birthday. The cops shout obscenities and shield their heads. Cameron and I want to preserve ourselves more than Walt Disney did, so we bolt for the safety of the ambulance – tossing out all previous ruminations about paramedics running.

Cameron slams open the sliding door and I follow in behind him. The cops are still dragging Omar by the shoulders like bodyguards navigating a celebrity criminal through a media scrum outside court. No one appears to have taken a hit, yet. The three extra bodies eventually pile into the rear of the ambulance and one of the cops bangs the door shut. We're safe. We all feel a bit like doomsday preppers hiding out in a bunker during a nuclear holocaust, and it's a tight fit. Between the stretcher, treatment desk and seats, there isn't much room left for comfort. Hard objects jab into soft flesh. It could be guns, truncheons, OC spray cannisters, stethoscopes, trauma scissors. I don't know and I don't want to remain compressed in this quarter-of-a-million-dollar sardine can any longer to find out. I swim through the bodies and make my way through the gap between the two front seats and climb into the driver's seat, freeing up some room in the back. Cameron manages to do the same and get into the passenger side.

Everyone manages to find somewhere to sit in our mobile magpie buffer, so I offer to drop the cops back to their car. We agree never to speak of this incident again and, out of pity, offer to drop Omar back to his house as well. He's thankful, but now he's panicking about how he's going to pay the fee for the ambulance. He doesn't have private health insurance or a concession card. When we arrive outside his house, he starts opening his wallet and offering us cash. We wave off his ridiculous gesture and tell him not to worry – we haven't done any treatment, so he won't receive a bill. I tell him he's lucky, though, for two reasons. Another pair of paramedics in a bad mood might have written up paperwork in a way that meant he'd have to pay for his absurd 000 call – but not us. We're in a good mood, now, not only because we escaped the demonic bird, but also because it turns out Omar's house is right next door to a coffee shop.

'That's my shop. I own it,' says Omar. 'Come in and I'll make you whatever you want.'

'*Alhamdulillah!*' says Cameron.

'What?' I reply.

'You're in Bankstown now, mate. Time to start learning Arabic.'

8

RUB (AND TUG) OF THE GREEN

'Got the job of the night for you, guys,' says the dispatcher through the radio, stifling a laugh. 'It's a pysch at the Male Wonderland.'

I know why. The words 'Male Wonderland' immediately conjure up an image of a seedy, underground gay sauna. And this is not where we're expecting to find ourselves, not least of all because this is the south-west. Those places only exist in the city, as far as I know.

It's the early hours of Monday morning, our first night shift of the week. So far we've assured someone that their hiccups weren't going to kill them, transported a lady to hospital because she was convinced a piece of cotton bud broke off in her ear and would permanently damage her hearing and fixed someone's broken sling strap. The dispatcher is enjoying our misfortune a lot more than we are, and we're contemplating a second hit of caffeine to get us through the second half of the shift, seeing as it's gearing up to be similar to the first half with the news we've just been given. But even though it sounds like it won't be serious, a brothel job is always, at the very least, entertaining.

We locate the address as a dark wooden door that hasn't had a new coat of paint since it was installed and is illuminated only by a flickering neon '31' above. It's nestled between a bakery and a pawnbroker in a shopping district. All the regular businesses have been closed since late yesterday afternoon, right as this one started gearing up for the night's activities. As we ease in against the gutter alongside the row of shops, there's no competition for a parking spot. No one is around this late at night. No one who isn't up to anything unwholesome, anyway.

Then a police patrol sedan slots in behind us. This is becoming a theme in the Bankstown area.

The dispatcher hadn't mentioned anything about the police when assigning us the job, so we're curious. The two cops get out and walk towards the driver's side of the ambulance. I wind my window down to see if they've got any idea what's going on. As I'm doing this, the mysterious door labelled '31' creaks inwards and a shifty-looking young Asian bloke sticks his head out from behind it. He beckons us over with a sense of urgency. I call out for him to wait until I talk to the police. With no other information other than we're here for a 28-year-old male in psychological distress, in a sex den, in the early hours of the morning, the situation doesn't represent the pinnacle of safety. We won't be rushing in to save the day just yet.

The cops tell us they've got no more information than us, just that they've been sent here blindly by their dispatcher as well. I alight from the ambulance to continue the conversation on the footpath. As soon as my feet hit the ground, the ambulance's data screens beeps behind me, so I turn to look at it. A new bar of text flashes on the display: *Caller states he paid for an hour session but only lasted 10 minutes and now wants his money back.*

I collapse onto the pavement with laughter.

This job has instantly taken the crown for the most ridiculous incident I've been involved in as a paramedic. I haven't even seen the patient yet, but it's already added another mark on the tally of bizarre sex- and genital-related patient issues that will continue to plague my career for years to come.

The two police officers approach as I'm attempting to compose myself and get back to my feet. They say they've just seen the updated information as well and it's okay if we want to leave. They can handle this one without our assistance.

I decline. There's no way I'm not going inside to witness this.

I've been a qualified paramedic in Bankstown for six months at this point. I've got the experience of being a leader of several major jobs under my belt, and my confidence in treating deathly sick patients has been building exponentially. I've injected medications into paediatrics that have saved them from their airways closing with seconds to spare. I've treated victims of housefires and major industrial accidents. I've trained several probationers and learned the necessities of a second language – I can say stuff like *hospital, allergy, pension and Medicare card,* and *can you walk?* in Arabic. But a corollary of this new-found confidence is that when faced with a ridiculous scenario, the only way I know how to approach it is to be equally as ridiculous myself. Dark humour and laughter are the only way to get through this job without giving yourself an aneurysm. Bleeding hearts have no ability to think critically, and so they just screw themselves over along with the patients they signed up to serve.

Before I wasn't rushing. Now I can't come to the aid of the concerned young gentleman peering out from behind number 31 fast enough. We follow him through the door of discretion, the kind of which are strewn throughout the south-west's industrial areas, advertising themselves only to those actively looking, and head up a dingy stairwell. At the top, the stairs open into a brightly lit reception area with a décor theme redolent of a cheap Chinese restaurant, complete with lanterns and, on the reception desk, one of those lucky cats with the swinging arm. The young dude, who I now figure to be the receptionist, implores us to engage with two figures arguing at the other end of the room. One is a woman, who instantly voids my gay sauna theory.

We're in a good, old-fashioned dodgy brothel for straight men.

As we approach the pair, I notice a hallway that runs off the middle of the reception area with closed doors recessed all the way along it. If there are any sounds emanating from them at this point, thankfully they're obscured by the unfolding dispute.

The young guy is of Middle Eastern origin and has limited English. His quarrel is with a significantly older, possibly pregnant, Caucasian working lady wearing a stained silk nightie. It doesn't cover what needs to be covered and I can't help but think she needs to start shopping in the maternity section. She's not wearing any makeup and undulating craters of acne keep me focused on her face so I can avoid the unwanted anatomy workshop that's happening lower down. She's probably around 50 years old, although I'm becoming experienced with characters with hard miles on them, so she could just as easily be in her mid-30s or 40s. At this point, however, it's just too hard to tell and too impolite to ask. I'm suspecting Tracy's services are for this establishment's more budget-conscious patrons.

The guy spots us.

'You . . . you help me,' he pleads, pointing towards me.

I have no idea how he expects me, a paramedic, to do that. But I'm here to play ball.

'No problem, sir, I'm going to help you,' I reply, putting two open-palmed hands up in front of me to indicate everything will be okay.

'This silly prick fucked me for about three minutes, shot his load everywhere, and now wants a refund because he couldn't last the whole hour,' says the courtesan through her remaining teeth. 'Then he just lost his shit when I told him no. Started screaming about Allah and demanding to use the phone. So bloody Jerry lets him,' she continues, motioning with disdain towards the receptionist, who's now looking sheepish.

The two female police officers are barely containing their laughter, while my partner Rhiannon is shaking her head and rolling her eyes. Partly because she doesn't want to be here dealing with this, and partly because she knows it's giving me ammunition to go full court-jester mode. She can't believe she's missing out on coffee for this crap. A fellow university pathway paramedic, Rhiannon is also just recently qualified and is wondering how all that money she's spent on a degree has landed her here: in a low-rent knock shop in Bankstown in the middle of the night, watching her partner gear up to do his best ACCC impersonation and pretend to help this punter get his money back.

The client continues to ramble in what is clearly a cocaine-fuelled combination of English and Arabic. I pick up a few key words that involve sex positions, financial amounts and titles of relatives, including his mother.

'Mate, this is a weird time and place to bring your mum into it. But leave this to me. I'll sort it out. Jerry!' I shout. 'We'll resolve this as quickly as possible but first we're going to need to do a full investigation. I'm talking price lists, client logs, CCTV footage – you happen to have that in the rooms? No? Alright, we're also going to need all the girls out here and I'm going to need to interview each one individually. This is crucial for the investigation. This is a serious matter, and we can't leave until there's a resolution.'

I'm talking fast and taking command in the only way I know how – based on what I've seen in American police movies. In my mind I'm like Chris Tucker in *Rush Hour.* Jerry, Tracy the prostitute and the client all look stunned. Jerry even begins shuffling some paperwork together to give to me. I guess when there's an official-looking person in uniform talking in an assertive manner, the average citizen becomes obsequious.

The police and Rhiannon see straight through the act, however.

'Mate, we'll sort this out. Go and help someone that needs an ambulance,' says one of the cops, with an amused headshake. The policewoman has clearly had her fill of the night's entertainment and just wants to get on with things. She's right; I've had my fun.

I abandon my temporary career change as a consumer rights advocate, hopeful that the issue will be resolved peacefully, and head back to the ambulance to see if the next case will provide amusement or affliction.

It could be both. Someone's grandmother has accidentally eaten an entire hash cookie.

Travis is pleading like a bad *Home and Away* actor in a death scene as he shakes his grandmother, Joan, by the shoulder: 'Wake up, Nan, wake up. Please!'

She's splayed out on an armchair. Travis is panicking; he thinks he's killed her.

When he's not accidentally knocking off grannies, the guy is quite the baker, it turns out. Though you won't find him supplying hot cross buns and Vegemite scrolls to the local Coles in Punchbowl. His customers don't buy in bulk, and he doesn't keep a ledger of his transactions. He knows his way around a set of kitchen scales, however. So when Joan got peckish in the wee small hours, she headed to the kitchen and found a jar that had been left out, containing her grandson's latest culinary creation. She was completely unaware it was part of a new side hustle and not practice for a *MasterChef* audition.

The guttural snore that reverberated through the house woke Travis and he instantly knew something was wrong with Gran. And spotting the open jar on the kitchen bench, he knew Joan had grabbed the wrong biscuit receptacle. So he called an ambulance immediately.

Travis's Gothic waif of a girlfriend, who hasn't had time to put pants on, or just isn't ashamed in front of strangers, is hovering nearby looking more amused than stressed.

'What do we do? What do we do?' Travis pleads.

He seems to be expecting us to crack out the defib.

'Tee up some cartoons on Foxtel and get a couple of kebabs ordered on Uber Eats for when she wakes up,' I say. 'It's just weed, mate. I think she'll pull through.'

'So it won't harm her, even though she's old?' Travis asks.

'Well, judging by her love of Pink Floyd and The Grateful Dead, I reckon this isn't Gran's first rodeo,' I say, pointing to a nearby record shelf. 'It's probably just been a while between blunts for her.'

'So you think she'll be fine?'

'She suffering from an acute case of total green-out, so I think she'll be really bloody hungry in a few hours. But other than that, yes, I think she'll be fine. I'll even check her blood pressure and oxygen levels for you.'

'She's got a bad heart, too.'

'Alright, I'll do an ECG as well. All part of the service.'

I unzip our kits and start attaching wires and probes, poking and prodding, looking for landmarks for electrodes and checking electronic readings on LCD screens. And all the readings are fine. Of course they are. It's just a bit of dope. But something isn't right with Joan. I can't work out what it is. It's bugging me because all her vitals are fine, and I've just promised Travis she'll be fine, too.

'Maybe we should take her to hospital, just to be safe,' I tell Travis.

There's nothing more embarrassing as a paramedic than admitting to a patient's family member that they were right, and you were wrong. Some verbal judo is needed now to get Travis back on side and restore confidence in me.

'But . . . but you said she was going to be fine. What's wrong with her?'

Travis is starting to panic again.

'Ever thought dreadlocks might be a good look, Joan?' calls Rhiannon from behind me.

I'm confused by the strange question. Rhiannon just motions back towards Joan. I see her mouth twitching and now I realise what it is I couldn't work out. The corners of Joan's mouth are quivering. She's stifling a goofy grin from forming. I must have woken her while checking her vitals, and in the funky and mellow mood she's in, she hasn't wanted to be disturbed anymore, so she's bunged on being asleep.

Now I've got to double-down by not taking Joan to hospital and backpedalling with Travis again. After all the fakers I've encountered, and there are many in the south-west that have required some creative trickery to expose their charade*, I've now been stumped by a stoned octogenarian.

'Morning, Joan,' I say. 'You don't want to go to hospital, do you?'

---

* Some people are so versed in and so committed to faking unconsciousness that the traditional methods of waking someone up are so futile it's not worth bothering. The trapezius squeeze or the sternal rub won't even elicit so much as a flinch in these professional pretenders. The most foolproof method of exposing an actor is by raising an arm above their head – because if someone is really out cold, their limp hand will slap them in the face. The act is exposed when they gently shift the falling limb to lay beside them to avoid smacking themselves. Another method is the nasopharyngeal airway (NPA), or 'truth trumpet' – a hollow rubber tube with a flared end that is inserted into a nostril and ends up in the posterior pharynx. This is an essential tool for providing oxygenation for someone with trismus (fancy word for lockjaw), also another favoured tactic of the faker, but commonly seen in seizures and head injuries. Most bluffers will tolerate this for about six seconds before they get sick of a pointy tube tickling their tonsils.

She shakes her head once without opening her eyes.

'Better put a bottle of Powerade on that Uber order, too,' I tell Travis. 'I reckon she'll be pretty thirsty.'

Joan opens one eye, winks at me and shuts it again as we walk out the door.

'Good thing you went to CSU,' I say to Rhiannon.

9

LOST IN TRANSLATION

Twelve months in Bankstown is enough to realise why no one wants to be sent here as their permanent appointment. It's not difficult work, but it's endlessly frustrating. The pace is non-stop, attending patient after patient, all day, all night, from start to finish of shift, with minimal downtime. Yet I can count the number of times I've had to radio the hospital, alerting them that we're bringing in a critical patient, on one hand. We should be doing this every job because every job should be an emergency. But they aren't.

From the thousands of patients I've attended to, hardly any have been in a critical condition. Rival bikie-gangs are trading lead-filled love letters like they're '90s Pokémon cards, but the only place I come close to seeing any action like this is watching it on the news on my days off. The newsreaders talk about the paramedics' desperate efforts* to save the victims, and I'm desperately wishing I was one of them. Everybody says the risk of PTSD is the biggest downside of being a paramedic, but I'm starting to think I'm in danger of discovering a new condition: lack of traumatic stress disorder.

Nights are always the worst. The silliest stuff comes out of Punchbowl, Greenacre, Riverwood and the other suburbs that surround Bankstown once the sun has gone down. Hardly anyone wants to go to hospital at night – which defeats the purpose of calling an ambulance. Nobody understands that an ambulance is a vehicle that gets you to hospital when you're in such a bad way that you can't make it there yourself. We go multiple nights in a row without transporting a single patient. We're seen as some sort of mobile GP and pharmacy because these services are closed at night.

This area doesn't just frustrate those of us stationed at Bankstown, but the rest of the paramedics in Sydney, too. We often get so busy we need to start dragging in ambulances from out of town to help cover the workload. Just because a patient doesn't end up going to hospital, doesn't mean they take up any less of our time. A stack of

* Often with major traumatic events, such as shootings and motor-vehicle accidents, there aren't really any desperate efforts. In fact, sometimes there's no effort at all. But it sounds better on the news to say that there was. Sometimes you simply can't resurrect someone because their injuries are so severe they are incompatible with being alive. However, that term upset a minor celebrity on Twitter once, despite it being a universally recognised medical term, so now we say 'un-survivable injuries' so that D-listers don't get their feelings hurt by reality.

paperwork needs to be completed for everyone who gets assessed, which is usually our only chance to rehydrate and eat something as well. So, while local crews are out of action, and the calls keep streaming in, ambulances from faraway suburbs get absorbed into the maelstrom.

In the south-west, we get a sick sense of schadenfreude whenever an ambulance crew that's used to servicing Dover Heights or Palm Beach pipes up on the radio. You can hear the annoyance in their sun-soaked voices, furious that their soy lattes might get cold and they might have to interact with a poor person or someone who doesn't speak English very well.

Tonight, we're pulled over in a dark street in Greenacre. The eerie stillness and lack of streetlights mean we've locked the doors. You wouldn't stop here at this time of night if you weren't wearing a uniform and didn't have a good reason for doing so – it's that kind of place. The ambulance's dome light is the only source of illumination, so anyone could sneak up on us from the blackness. I'm tapping away on the laptop we use to complete case sheets. It's a sturdy device with an exterior that could withstand a drone strike from the US military, but with software that's as dependable as a politician in a disaster. Rhiannon and I are back working another roster together and she's bopping away in the driver's seat to the appropriately tuned WSFM. Bruce Springsteen is crooning about dancing in the dark, but I can't imagine his muse was a sleep-deprived paramedic in a sketchy Greenacre cul-de-sac.

I'm entering the vital signs of a patient we just left at home into our non-transport case sheet. Jade's a pregnant 19-year-old who's becoming a bit of a regular. She called us tonight for nausea, which is what she's called for every night this week. When we suggested nausea was part of the deal with pregnancy, as opposed to a medical emergency, she fired up and insisted we're obliged to give her a Zofran shot because of our duty of care to treat her symptoms. We said we're happy to do this the first couple of times but told her that she now needs to get a script for Zofran from her GP, as opposed to tying up an ambulance whenever her tummy gets upset.

'I can't afford to pay for a box of this myself!' she yells.

'Well, if you can't afford a box of medication, you certainly can't afford the bills for all these ambulances you're calling. And you definitely won't be able to afford to raise a child,' comes Rhiannon's retort.

'I PAY YOUR TAXES AND I'M ON A PENSION! SO I GET TO CALL WHENEVER I WANT FOR ZOFRAN!'

Rather than point out the factual inaccuracy of Jade's statement, we give her the Zofran and leave. We'll deal with the bung when it comes in next week.

I finish scribbling my electronic signature at the end of the case sheet when a frenzied call of distress barks through the radio speaker.

'Code One! Code One!' cries the distressed voice.

Nothing, not even an amphetamine-laced Red Bull solution mainlined straight into the external jugular vein, can wake up a paramedic like the call of a Code 1. It means there's a colleague in immediate danger and they need help, preferably the armed kind, urgently.

It's a crew from one of the beachy areas that begrudgingly ventured into the south-west vortex earlier in the evening. They obviously didn't escape and now they may not at all. While keying the commands into his computer to inform the nearest police units, our dispatcher must've caught a glimpse of the dot on his screen that represents our car.

'Guys, I'll get you to help with this Code One as well,' says the dispatcher. 'You're right on top of them and will be closer than the cops.'

'Copy,' we reply. 'Just give us the address and we'll be right there.'

There's always a small delay while our data screens drop down information from the great ambulance controllers in the sky, so the dispatcher voices the address and Rhiannon's foot hits the floor so quickly it flings the unrestrained laptop into my chest. I catch my breath and stuff the computer into a nook beside me. I've barely managed to put my seatbelt on when Rhiannon screeches around a corner and we see the work lights of the ambulance belonging to our distressed friends about halfway down another dark street. It's boxed in by a ring of cars. Even if the crew could retreat to the ambulance from the house, there'd still be no escape. Not only does this look bad, but it also looks like we're outnumbered.

Rhiannon and I haven't discussed, or had time to think about, what we're walking into. We're on autopilot again and have disregarded our own safety to help our mates. Few paramedics would do any differently.

Bounding up the front lawn towards the house, armed with only a radio and a very questionable blue belt in jiu-jitsu, I hear the words *Yallah!* and *Habibi!* loudly zinging around the inside of the house. These words are used in the Arabic world in many contexts, the meaning of which is entirely dependent on the emotion backing them: happiness, sadness, fear, anger, joy, disgust. Anything could be at play here and I'm about to find out exactly what – safety and self-preservation disregarded entirely.

And then I see about 30 people crammed into the front room. Large, imposing men. But also people who look like their wives. And children. And parents. All ages, shapes and sizes. Two paramedics are knelt on the floor, with the crowd ringed around them, surrounding them like the cars on the street are surrounding the ambulance.

But no one is attacking anyone. No one is injured. Or being held hostage. No one is even being yelled at. Sure, some of the voices are loud. But the over-zealous emotion isn't directed at the paramedics. Various family members are communicating expressively with each other with words and phrases and hand gestures I don't understand. The two paramedics are very much unharmed and reassuring an upset-looking lady on the couch, and their expressions go from nervous to relieved when they spot us entering the room.

'Hey guys, what's happening?' I ask tentatively, wondering what made these guys activate the Bat-Signal.

'Well, we were called to this lady for shortness of breath,' one of the out-of-area ambos tells me. 'We were starting to assess her when all of a sudden all these people turned up and were yelling and screaming and we got super worried, so we called for the cops. We thought we were in danger.'

'Ah, you guys aren't from around here, are you?'

'Nope. Northern Beaches.'

'Oh, well welcome to Bankstown,' I say, completely cognisant of what is transpiring now. 'We can probably call off the police, then.'

'Police?' says one of the Arabic men. 'What we need police for, brother?'

'Police? *Police?*' others start asking a bit louder, agitated by the prospect.

'No, no. No police. No police. *Shway shway,*' I tell the crowd, motioning with my hands that everything is alright and showing off my knowledge of the Arabic phrase for *take a chill pill.*

The crowd bursts out laughing.

'Ahahaha. *Shway shway. Shway shway,*' they say, holding their stomachs as they chortle.

It's always a crowd-pleaser and tension-breaker, particularly when delivered in an atrocious Australian accent.

The Northern Beaches ambos laugh along nervously, too.

'Don't stress, guys,' I tell our colleagues. 'This happens at just about every job in the Bankstown area. Whenever someone is in trouble, someone hits a speed dial button and then a distress call goes out to every family member in a 50-kilometre radius, much like our Code One call, and somehow everyone usually gets here quicker than we do.'

'Yes, this is correct, brother,' another of the men says. 'When there's emergency in family, we all hurry as quickly as possible.'

'I don't know how you guys do it,' I say. 'But you should oversee dispatching ambulances. I've been first on the scene at car accidents and I'll turn away for 30 seconds and next thing I know, every cousin, uncle and stepsibling of the patient has turned up.'

'Yes, this is secret we cannot tell. Come, brother, let me make Arabic coffee for all of you. Very strong. Good for your job, I think.'

'I'll have one if you're having one, brother,' I say, trying to form some cool linguistic bond, but instead just sounding like the whitest dude in the world.

The Northern Beaches paramedics don't look so sure.

'You always make sure they have one with you,' I say. 'That's how you know they're not poisoning you.'

The crowd laughs again.

The patient, Zeinab, is looking relaxed now as well. Plenty of clues hint at this being an emotional episode, as is so common in the south-west. My spider-sense is becoming more finely tuned to quick diagnostics, much like I used to revere Big Phil's ability to do. But I want to make sure there's nothing else going on. I sit down with my tiny porcelain cup of piping-hot Turkish coffee and ask if anything has upset our patient tonight.

'Yes, brother, she get this message from overseas just now,' one of the men says as he shoves a mobile phone at me.

I choke on the sip of coffee I've just taken.

'Holy . . . shit . . .' I splutter between coughs.

Playing on the screen is a poorly filmed video of a terrified man sitting on a chair with a hood over his head and his hands and feet hog-tied. A large black flag with white symbols is draped behind him, and two men wearing balaclavas stand guard either side. One with an AK-47 and one with a machete.

I signal for the phone to be taken away. I don't want to see where the rest of the footage goes.

'Her cousin,' the man says.

'Is that . . . is that ISIS?' I ask.

'Yes,' he replies. 'Very bad people.'

I feel like asking if the cousin has gotten mixed up with the wrong crowd, but this expression seems flippant.

'Is he okay?' I ask.

I have no idea what to say.

'No, brother.'

The man makes a cutting motion with one finger across the front of his neck. Zeinab bursts into tears. All four of us paramedics stare at each other. Rhiannon and I might be the Bankstown locals, but we've never come across anything like this before. We're speechless. It's another south-west idiosyncrasy and there's no page of the paramedic playbook we can pull from to treat this one. So we play the only card we have left when faced with situations like this and offer the patient a trip to hospital. It's the Get Out of Jail Free card for paramedics. There's certainly no medical issue for a doctor to solve, but it's reassuring to the patient that there's further assessment that can be done for symptoms like shortness of breath and chest pain. And there might at least be someone with more psychiatric training than us who might have an idea what to say.

We offer to take Zeinab in our ambulance, so that the Northern Beaches guys can make a run for their sea-breezed suburbs while they complete their paperwork. They can't accept fast enough and leave their Turkish coffees sitting on the table, still steaming, not a sip taken.

10

WILD WILD SOUTH-WEST

A mild degree of mental instability is a prerequisite for being a paramedic. Who else, besides cops, would drive with such charged enthusiasm towards reports of gunfire? And let's not delve into the psychological requirements for joining that profession.

When someone's been shot, that's all we know. How many times? Whereabouts? With what sort of gun? Is there still an active shooter on the scene? Are there more victims? We know the answer to none of these questions. Incidents of this calibre are flung through the airwaves to the data terminal of the nearest ambulance before the panicked caller has barely finished answering the 000 operator's question about which town or suburb they're in. Our job notes give us nothing. All we know is that we're pelting like greyhounds off the line to the biggest job of our careers.

'Bit early for kung fu, isn't it?' says my partner, Chad, quoting Eric Bana's *Chopper*.

He's hopping up and down on his seat with excitement. I can almost see him salivating with Pavlovian conditioning. Chad's got adult ADHD and often forgets to take his medication. Or runs out because of his penchant for sharing it with his mates. Nothing breaks his focus when treating a deathly ill patient, but between incidents he's a hyperactive toddler constantly spouting movie quotes, macabre jokes and song lyrics that he'll always find a way to substitute his own name into.

'We need a tune for this,' he says, flicking through a Spotify playlist that's hooked into the ambulance via Bluetooth.

'Aah, a classic. The Joker and the Chad,' he says, bastardising the title of Wolfmother's *Joker and the Thief*.

The electric opening riff fills the cockpit and I remember reading somewhere how rock music makes men subconsciously drive faster. No extra encouragement is needed today, however. We're racing because we don't want anyone else to get the jump on us and steal the job away. Only shootings and stabbings have the miraculous ability to awaken paramedics who've said they can't respond because they need to use the bathroom or replace faulty equipment.

We take the final turn onto the street we're after, having completely forgotten that we're supposed to stage ourselves blocks away for safety until the police confirm they're on scene. But luckily for us, if there's one thing that's guaranteed in the south-west, it's that the cops always arrive first. Their cars are much faster and their numbers far greater than ours.

A swarm of human activity is buzzing ahead at the end of the street, in a large grass courtyard that's ringed by a U-shaped block of at least 100 multi-storey public housing units. Blue lights flash from hastily parked cars, voices bark commands across the mayhem. A television crew is already setting up its cameras and lights, and I make a mental note to watch my language this time. The only other place I've seen so many cops is when they show academy-graduation footage on the news.

Fretting officers encourage us over to an area where a smaller group of cops is converged around a body in the courtyard, some kneeling, some standing. Others are already poking around for evidence, holding back bystanders, taking statements and stringing up crime scene tape.

One police officer is doing frantic CPR on the victim, but Chad takes over. The adrenaline surge the officer was obviously feeling made him push way too hard and fast*.

* This treatment is an anachronism – we no longer do CPR on patients who have gone into cardiac arrest due to a traumatic cause, such as being stabbed, shot or hit by a car. It's incredible that only very recently, medical boffins realised that CPR is detrimental in these cases. It's very simple when you think about it: CPR makes the heart pump blood around the body's blood vessels when it's stopped doing that by itself. So when a patient is full of holes that are leaking, gushing or spurting blood, continuing to operate the pump will only make whatever blood is left in the pipes exit the holes much faster. Instead, we now focus first on patching up the holes with dressings and tourniquets, then restoring missing blood volume, before starting CPR. It's no surprise that survival rates of traumatic cardiac arrests are practically zero.

It isn't a regularly drilled skill for them like it is for us, and Chad settles into a steadier, calmer rhythm. I force my way into the throng and come across a waxy body encircled by sticky red blood. Great pools of the stuff stain the grey concrete path where this man has fallen and for a moment I consider asking Chad whether we should just pronounce him dead now. There's so much claret I can see boot prints from where the police have had to stand to get near the patient. Then I think, what the hell, how often do you get to try to resuscitate someone who's been shot?

I kneel next to the man's head and start unzipping the oxygen bag to grab a suction unit, so I can remove the blood that's swishing around in his oropharynx before I can start using a bag mask to refill his lungs with oxygen.

'Watch where you step!' a cop yells at me. 'We need to preserve the evidence.'

I look across and see I've just kicked away a shell casing.

'Sorry,' I say sheepishly.

I haven't got time to dwell on this ignominious mistake though. I need to clear the man's airway with haste if we're to have any chance of getting him back. His dead eyes stare up at me as the maroon fluid slurps out of his throat and up the suction tubing like a pre-mix soda gun in reverse. Residents leer from upper-floor balconies while we work on the patient, some heckling and jeering like they're clinging to the side of the Thunderdome and those of us down below are the afternoon's grisly entertainment. I'm deaf to what they're saying, looking down the patient's airway like it's the lens of a telescope.

I start to wonder where exactly the wounds are, so I stare further down the man's body and see two fleshy perforations – one on the inside of a bicep and one in the lower abdomen. There could be more, but there's no time to go searching because this airway is still extensively contaminated. And you can't live if you don't have an airway.

My focus snaps back to the wider environment when a doctor from a medical retrieval team that's just arrived taps me on the shoulder.

'Mind if I take over?' he says.

I can't give up my position quickly enough. This airway is one for the experts. The patient will need intubation, whereby a breathing tube is inserted through the vocal cords and into the lungs, and then an inflatable cuff will prevent any further interference from blood in the ventilation process. I leave the doctor to his domain and turn my focus to finding IV access. Thankfully the patient still has engorged veins sitting proudly on his skin like well-fed green slugs. Using the biggest needle I can find, I poke into a vessel on the arm that doesn't have a bullet hole in it – size equals speed in the intravenous game. And speed is good when you've run out of blood. The critical care paramedic who's working with the doctor hands me a pump set and a bag of O negative to attach to the cannula.

'Squeeze that as fast as you can and don't stop until it's empty. Then I'll give you another one,' he says.

I pump the squishy bag of plasma like a strangely pertinent stress ball. My hand soon cramps from the constant squeezing so I start alternating. The doctor has his breathing tube in situ and is now pushing oxygen back into the man's lungs. He needs to perform a second procedure, though, and so he hands control of the now-secured airway to Chad. The cops help us out by rotating through rounds of CPR. The doc unsheathes a scalpel from a pouch in his pants and starts slicing into the patient's side, in between his ribs. It's a barbaric procedure called a thoracostomy which releases air and blood that's gotten trapped between the lungs and the inner chest wall, which can stop the lungs from re-inflating properly. The hole isn't big enough to allow adequate drainage, so the doc jams a finger in it and begins to sweep in a circular motion to increase its diameter. Everyone squirms and winces. A cop turns away to vomit.

Now all we can do is wait. Ventilate, circulate and wait. The first bag of blood runs dry. So does the second. And the third. Nothing changes. No pulses return. No spontaneous breaths are taken. And we're out of blood. Hope is gone and the doctor evaluates the situation.

'Anyone think of anything we haven't tried?' he asks the group.

Head shakes all round.

'Anyone have any objections to ceasing resuscitation, then?'

Same response.

Okay, time of death . . .

Everyone backs away in a quiet retreat, careful not to inadvertently punt away any more evidence. This place doesn't belong to us anymore; it's a crime scene owned by the forensics guys now.

The voices on the balconies fall silent when they see us start to walk away. They know what it means. The act of professionals attempting a resuscitation always gives a glint of hope, no matter how false or futile it may be. But when the pros quit, it's like a morose mic drop. The onlookers realise one of their neighbours is dead. And not of old age or a medical episode, but a savagely violent crime that could just as easily taken out one of them had they been in the wrong place at the wrong time.

As I'm carrying equipment back to the ambulance, I pass a police officer taking a statement from a resident. The bystander is livid, animatedly recounting what he saw. He points in the direction that he saw the shooter flee and then explains the reason behind the act.

It's not a targeted gangland drive-by, and there's no burnt-out getaway car smouldering three suburbs away, as is so characteristic of an incident like this in our area. No, it was just a simple neighbourly courtyard dispute over a packet of cigarettes. An illegal handgun went off. Two men entered; one man left.

The debrief and clean-up lasts for hours, which is one way to speed up a shift. But there's still half a day left, and it's going to feel strange standing in the lounge room of the next non-emergency patient while a news update flashes across their TV, broadcasting us trying to revive the victim of a daylight shooting in the local area.

My vision is a false premonition, though, because just as the medical retrieval team is about to depart our station for the airport hangar they're based out of, our control centre calls and requests we partner up again. Somebody is drowning at the beach.

'Beach? There's no beach in Bankstown,' scoffs the doctor in his Irish accent.

Judging from his profession and nationality, Chad and I deduce that this registrar likely resides in County Coogee or The Republic of Bondi and isn't familiar with the natural wonders that lie west of Anzac Parade.

'Oh, but there is, doctor,' says Chad. 'Revesby Beach.'

Beach is a misnomer for the one-metre-wide strip of sand that's both not in Revesby (it's in Picnic Point) and is essentially just a clearing on the Georges River with a boat ramp for jetski enthusiasts. You won't find any English backpackers trying to brown their pasty complexions on the shore or any muscled lifeguards saving distressed tourists as they thrash about in rips. At best you might see some bored young ladies with fake eyelashes staring at their phones over their botoxed lips while their boyfriends spray rooster tails of water on them from their Sea-Doos.

That's why we presume someone's ill-fated stunt has come to an abrupt stop on meeting with a tree branch hanging low over the riverbanks. Then an updated note hits the data terminal:

Caller states saw someone struggling while swimming in the river. Caller no longer on scene.

'Good thing they've stuck around to help,' I say with sarcasm.

'Mate, good riddance, I say,' says Chad. 'Nothing worse than when you get one of these muppets who has just done a first aid course try to tell you how to do your job. I've peeled my badge off before and handed it to one of them and told them to run the show if they know it all. Should've seen how quickly the bloke shut up.'

We dart through the suburbs and arrive at the turn-off to the south-west's most popular swimming hole. We bump and bounce down the undulating dirt road that leads to the water, feeling the shock of every eroded crevice through the Sprinter's over-inflated tyres and hard suspension. The entry flattens out into a glade, and we motor another 100 metres or so to the boat ramp, where we line up in a vee with the retrieval ambulance, overlooking the water. Both crews dismount their respective vans to the tranquil silence of a riverside summer afternoon. Silence because there's nobody here. No one is flailing in the water. No one is backing in a trailer behind a fully optioned dual-cab ute. And there's definitely no one who looks like they called an ambulance flagging us down.

Two police sedans kick up dust behind us as they hammer down the dirt track. A steadily increasing drone above signals that the police chopper is imminent. We know there's specially trained rescue paramedics on the way, as well as one of our inspectors and, no doubt, police divers. But all for what looks like it's going to be either a body retrieval or a hoax.

With the assistance of the highway patrolmen, we scour what we can of the water from the shore, but we all know we're searching for a ghost. Staring into the watery abyss isn't going to miraculously make someone appear or float to the surface. We finally give up and ask the dispatcher if he can ring back the caller and get more information.

'I can do you one better,' he says. 'The caller says he's going to come back and meet you.'

More emergency resources begin arriving, and I think to myself that this caller better have a good story to tell, or he's going to have some very unimpressed first responders to deal with.

After 10 minutes or so, a lone white Toyota Prius trundles down the dirt road. It stops short of the congregation and an overweight, balding man steps out. The sight he sees is no doubt intimidating. He must feel like he's stepped onto the set of a Michael Bay film; before him stands a semi-circle of ambulances, police and fire trucks, complete with a chopper circling overhead. And all the occupants are staring right at him.

He begins to stutter, but nothing of sense comes out. Chad volunteers himself as our spokesman.

'What the hell's going on, mate?' he says loudly. 'Where's this person who's drowning? And where did you bugger off to when you called it in?'

'I . . . I . . . I saw someone struggling to swim. And I thought they might get themselves into trouble. So I called 000. I . . . I certainly didn't think it would cause this much of a fuss,' he says with a sweeping hand motion across the plethora of uniformed men and women, who are standing in front of their vehicles with their arms crossed.

'This *fuss* is what happens when you say someone is drowning in the river, pal. Why didn't you hang around?' Chad continues.

'Well, I just thought it was better to be safe. It wasn't like it was an *emergency.* And I wanted to go and get a coffee.'

'A coff . . . what the . . . mate, someone could have drowned, and it was more important to you to go and get a coffee?'

Chad is livid, his face close to the boil.

'Well . . . well I didn't exactly see the person struggling. I just, kind of, *heard them.* I thought they would just send a lifeguard or something.'

'A lifeguard? What do you think this is? *Bondi Rescue*? There's no lifeguards around here. You call 000 and you get us. And what do you mean you just heard them?'

'There was this . . . splashing sound. It really sounded like someone was in trouble.'

'YOU MEAN YOU NEVER ACTUALLY SAW ANYONE DROWNING?'

'Well, I mean, I . . .'

A look of shame and guilt creeps across the man's face. Then everyone present interrupts the rest of the man's drivel with a collective 180-degree turn before he can continue. Something has disturbed the still water of the river. An abrupt splosh lasting less than a second.

Chad turns slowly back around, his voice building to a furious crescendo.

'OH MY GOD IT WAS A FUCKING *DUCK*, WASN'T IT?'

The man says nothing.

'Thanks for being a triple-zero hero, pal,' Chad says. 'I'll see if I can organise the keys to the city for you.'

Chad shakes his head and walks back to the group, leaving the man looking stunned. This fool hasn't a clue about the nature of the job we'd just been to before this. And he's also unaware of how he's just become the personification of the peculiar dichotomy that is being a paramedic in Bankstown.

11

PULLING TEETH

You are responding to a patient with a toothache at the dentist.

We double check the data screen to make sure we've read it right. We have.

'If we make it to this one, then I've seen everything,' says Chad. 'There is nothing that can get any dumber than this.'

'There's always something dumber,' I say.

'We haven't even got time to do our own job, let alone everyone else's. I mean, *fark*, what are they even expecting us to do?' he says with increasing frustration. 'Who's even made the call here, the patient or the dentist?'

The normally affable Chad must be getting hangry, a frequent and unavoidable emotional by-product of shift work. He's nearing the summit of Mount Meltdown. It's understandable.

'Surely not the dentist,' I reply.

'Thanks for coming, guys. I had no other choice but to call you,' says the dentist when we arrive.

Chad and I give each other the look, quickly enough so the dentist doesn't see it.

There's always a choice.

'The patient has come in for an extraction, but, well, we haven't made it that far,' the dentist continues, leading us past his reception desk and down the hallway to his rooms.

The clinic is a washout of white walls, bright lights and rich, bleachy aromas. The sights and smells of hygiene. A pleasant change to our usual work environment and a point in the redemption column for the dentist. It doesn't stop me placing our 15kg defibrillator on a chair just a little more loudly than necessary, though.

'This is Jaxton,' he says, introducing a male of around 30 years, outstretched on the chair of the dental engine.

Ultrasonically cleansed instruments lay unused on a tray hovering above Jaxton's lap. Suction hoses and water nozzles poke up beside them in a similar state of stasis. A bright overhead light remains on and points directly at Jaxton's face, framing it like a halo.

''Allo, gentsss.' Jaxton slurs at us in what sounds like a fake Cockney accent and drool appears in the corner of his mouth. There's something oddly familiar about his speech.

'He's not actually British,' the dentist informs us. 'It's just every time I try to get near his infected tooth, he squeals and pulls away. I've given him as much sedation as I can, which is when he started talking like this.'

Sedation. That's it. The familiar drowsy drawl of someone high on happy gas. We use a drug called methoxyflurane* frequently, which works similarly to the nitrous oxide favoured by dentists, and it's often known to not only make people completely forget that they're in pain, but also speak and behave in unusual ways. Jaxton seems pretty content right now, so the issue is unclear.

'Watch this,' says the dentist, picking up one of the shiny silver instruments from the tray. 'Jaxtonnn . . . we're going to get that tooth out now.'

He leans in towards Jaxton's dozy grin. It rapidly turns to horror and recoil. Jaxton tries to scarper backwards up the length of the chair, far away from the dentist's torture device, as though he's a World War II surgeon about to operate without anaesthesia, all the while emitting mouse-like squeaks.

'Oh god. Oh god,' exclaims Jaxton.

'Just call me Chad,' grunts Chad.

Chad loves a dad joke, and the best thing about this job for an amateur comedian is that they can use the same material every day on a different audience.

'See? I can't get near him,' says the dentist. 'And I'm maxed out on everything I can give him to relax. It's the worst case of dentophobia I've ever seen.'

---

* AKA the infamous green whistle.

'So, let me get this right,' I begin. 'He's got an infected tooth, which is causing him pain?'

'Yes.'

'He can keep taking pain relief for it, but ultimately it needs to be extracted, right?'

'Correct.'

'So he's come to a dentist to have the extraction performed?'

'Which is where we are now.'

'I'm very much aware of that. But he's so afraid of the dentist that every time you go near him to work on the tooth, he has a total breakdown and won't let you perform the procedure. So you've given him a tonne of sedation and now you want to get rid of him since you still can't take the tooth out and you can't very well kick him out onto the street because he's stoned off his tits?

'Well . . .'

'So you've called an emergency ambulance and made it our problem. And now we're going to have to take him to hospital, a place that doesn't do routine dentistry procedures like tooth extractions, and when he's seen by an actual medical doctor in a few hours, he will be referred to someone who does do tooth extractions. Someone like, I don't know, *a dentist.*'

'I . . . well . . . I . . . what else was I supposed to do?'

I lower my head in defeat because he's right. And I don't have the answer. All I know is that this sums up being a paramedic – we're the perennial receivers of handballs from one carer to another when a problem lands in the too-hard basket.

'You happen to catch any of that, Jaxton?' I call over to him.

'You're tay-ing me to 'ospital,' he drools, calm as he was when we first arrived.

'Afraid so, buddy. Guess that toothache will be hanging round a little longer. Grab the stretcher for us, would you, Chad? Don't want him falling over and chipping a tooth.'

Chad returns with the trolley and we wheel Jaxton through the waiting room of the dental surgery. He tips his head to a man sitting on one of the chairs and offers a cheery '*Guvna*'. We load Jaxton into the van. Chad lets out a sigh from the driver's seat.

'Happy?' he says in the universal way an ambulance driver asks if their partner in the back is ready to start driving to hospital.

'Haven't been happy in years, mate,' I reply, getting my dad-joke revenge.

Chad is crunching down a protein bar and giving me a speech about anabolic windows and being in ketosis. We've just finished having another turn in the cycle of stupidity and assisted Jaxton into a wheelchair, where Chad proceeded to push him over to a spot in front of the TV in the ED's waiting room where he could happily sit squawking at the other patients until his nitrous dream wore off. Eventually a doctor will arrive and look at him blankly with the same stunned expression we did before delivering the bad news.

We're sitting in the front of the ambulance and I'm in disbelief that I'm even required to type up this medical record. I'm about to give up midway through and finish it off later when a middle-aged woman and a guy of about 25, who I can only presume to be her son, pull up in a car across from us and walk towards the ambulance. Nothing good, or sensible, ever comes out of people approaching an ambulance, especially when it's parked right outside a hospital. From the sway of the approaching woman's gait, I've already named her Karen in my head and decided her son still lives at home with her. Chad sees the incoming threat and is quicker than me at making a tactical retreat. Not only that, he's in the mood for a stitch-up as well.

'Got to go to the toilet, mate. Oh, hi there. This lovely gentleman will help you,' he says to the woman, then jumps out of the ambulance.

Shit. I'm trapped.

'Hi there,' I say.

'My son needs a CT scan, what should I do?' she says abruptly.

'Er . . .' I reply, looking at the entrance to the hospital that's less than five metres away.

'No, that's no good. They refuse to do it.'

'Well, unfortunately we haven't got a CT scanner in the back of this thing, either,' I say, looking back into the rear compartment of the van as if it's a possibility. 'What's wrong with him?'

'His GP says it's a sinus infection, but it's not that. I know it's not.'

'Why has he told you it's a sinus infection?'

'Because Johnathon's had pain in the back of his nose the last few days.'

'That's it? Pain in his nose?'

'Yes.'

'The way he's sniffing and all congested, it sounds like a sinus infection to me too.'

'Why does everyone keep saying that? It's not a sinus infection. He needs a CT scan to figure out what it is.'

He doesn't.

'Look, I can understand why the emergency department won't do a CT scan. You realise it costs a lot of money to do one of those? So they reserve doing them for serious cases, like people having strokes and traumatic head injuries. You can always get a referral to a private imaging clinic.'

'And pay with my own money? You think I'm stupid? That's not the reason this place won't do a CT at all. The head of this hospital is a part-owner of most of the private clinics around here, that's why they'll only refer Johnathon on – to make more money for themselves.'

This woman is a chain made entirely of missing links.

'Okay, sorry, but I've got emergencies to get to,' I inform her. 'I can't hang around and debate conspiracy theories about the public health system with you.'

'What about if I go home and call an ambulance?'

'Why would you do that? You're at a hospital.'

'Yes, but if Johnathon comes back in an ambulance, they might do the CT scan.'

'I can guarantee you they won't. I'll even bet my house on it. That's not what ambulances are for. Please don't use up an ambulance for this. You're not going to get a CT scan for a sore nose in a public hospital emergency department for a completely healthy 25-year-old.'

'How can you be so uncaring? Why doesn't anybody . . .'

'Chad. CHAD! *CHAD!*' I scream. To be honest, I've got no idea where he's buggered off to. This is one of his greatest larks. He's still nowhere to be seen. 'Sorry, love. I've got to go. We've got an emergency.'

I'm left with no choice. It's time to break out the launch codes and hit the red button. I reach over and flick the switch that activates the siren. The wail is so loud under the awning of the ambulance bay, it could kickstart a dead heart. At the very least, it's splitting Karen's eardrums.

'AAAAHHHH,' she screams, covering her ears.

Johnathon just stands there with a vacant stare. Chad finally emerges to see what all the noise is about. He jumps back into the driver's seat. 'What's going on?'

'Just drive. *DRIVE!*'

He knows I won't ask again so he screeches out of the ambulance bay, leaving Karen and Johnathon standing in the car park with stunned expressions on their faces.

'You owe me a beer, you prick,' I say to Chad.

*

The dispatcher must see the dot that represents our ambulance speeding across his computer screen.

'Car 6890, looks like you guys are ready for your next job,' comes the voice through the radio.

We're not. I still haven't finished the paperwork for Jaxton, but right now I'll take anything as long as it gets me away from the ambulance bay where no doubt the wild Karen is still lurking, ready to pounce on the next unsuspecting ambulance crew.

'Send it through,' I reply.

'Traumatic injury in Villawood for you.'

'Detention centre?' asks Chad.

'Yep.'

There are only one of two places an ambulance is going if the suburb we're tasked to is Villawood. And neither of them is good news. Especially if the job description is traumatic injury. This time we won't be dealing with the aftermath of a brawl in a public housing block, however. We're headed to the infamous Villawood Detention Centre. Where we could still be dealing with the aftermath of a brawl.

Buried behind factories and warehouses in an industrial area, Villawood Detention Centre isn't some faraway island penitentiary as the images conjured by occasional news reports would suggest. It's only 20 kilometres west of Sydney's CBD, and within its towering fences and thick walls it houses a variety of characters including visa overstayers, asylum seekers and deplorably dangerous criminals awaiting deportation. Consequently, this diverse group brings a wide range of ambulance work as well. However, given the on-site medical centre and staff, if an ambulance has been called, it's usually because somebody has been maimed. Or maimed themselves. Unless it's the middle of the night and someone's asthma puffer has run out and there's no other option because the medical centre is shut.

Chad and I are prepared to walk into a full-blown lockdown. We're visualising resuscitating someone in a cell because they've been shanked in the guts or had their head stomped on. Security will form a protective ring around us as the rest of the inmates lose their collective shit – riots or copycat attacks aren't uncommon as soon as one person hits the deck. We know this all too well from previous experience. Treating a patient becomes exponentially more difficult when you're constantly looking over your shoulder, wondering if you'll make it out or end up being taken hostage.

Chad winds down his window at a boom gate and hits a buzzer announcing our arrival to the security staff. We head on through and wait in the sally port for the obligatory vehicle inspection – an always comical endeavour because, hey, what could we possibly be bringing in: sharp things and prohibited substances? Satisfied, the guard directs us to follow the road around to the medical centre where we'll find our patient.

'Medical centre? It can't be too bad if this guy's managed to get himself to the medical centre,' says Chad.

*

'It's really not too bad,' says Hassan in a thick Middle Eastern accent.

Hassan's an unassuming, middle-aged Assyrian man, displaced by conflict in his homeland and seeking refuge in a more peaceful society. Through the oscillations of worldly travel and mercurial geopolitics, his journey has hit a purgatorial terminus that sees him now an indefinite resident of a communal unit in Villawood. It's a complex situation and it makes me glad that I've chosen a job where the resolutions we offer are far more clear-cut.

I'm looking down at a hospital transfer document handed to me by the on-site nurse, who's just as confused as we are and extremely apologetic.

'I really didn't think we needed to get you guys, but you know what these doctors are like, they make up their minds and that's it,' he says to me.

'Oh, I know. What's worse is that once a doctor decides someone has to go to hospital, we have to take them. It's a protocol we've got to follow.'

'I'm sorry. I tried to say no,' Hassan tells me. 'I've never been in an ambulance. You call one in my country and they ask you for cash before they even get out of their van.'

'No need to apologise, mate,' I say.

The document tells me that Hassan had been playing soccer with some other residents when he was struck in the head by the ball from a stray kick. He wasn't knocked out or anything untoward. He felt slightly dizzy so he went to the medical centre. It was likely the most excitement the on-site doctor had had all day. The on-site doctor who's no longer around to tend to his patient. But felt the need to call an ambulance.

'He was worried about an intercranial bleed,' says the nurse. 'He wants him to go to hospital for a CT scan to rule it out.'

'What is it with senior medical personnel ordering an ambulance for the goofiest things today?' says Chad.

'And people wanting CT scans,' I say. 'I don't get it. It's not like Hassan is high-risk. He's not old and decrepit. He's not even on blood thinners, is he?'

I look through the medications listed in Hassan's paperwork. No anticoagulants are listed, only some recently commenced pills for high blood pressure and cholesterol. *The only win he's going to get in this place*, I think. I figure GP services in Hassan's homeland aren't as accessible and conducive to longevity as they are here. He's far from the most salubrious looking bloke too, repercussions of a hard lifestyle and a cultural diet that's not exactly in sequence with a robust cardiac constitution. Had he not been recently put on daily beta blockers and statins, he'd probably be dead of a heart attack in a few years.

Everything else about Hassan checks out fine, too. His vital signs are normal. He hasn't been copiously vomiting or having seizures. His pupils aren't darting off in different directions. There's no blood coming out of his ears or anything else to indicate a head injury. Anything to indicate something besides a grown man being hit in the head with a soccer ball.

'Honestly, if we sent a crew to everyone who went down after being hit in the head with a soccer ball, there'd be no ambulances left for anyone else,' I say. 'We'd be too busy carting off everyone in the A-League who feels like taking a dive.'

'Yeah, mate. What would a doctor know, anyway?' says Chad. 'They only *practice* medicine.'

Chad gets the final dad joke.

12
OFF THE CHOOK

His face turns from pink to red to white to purple to blue. The blue of a body ravenous for oxygen. The blue of millions of tiny capillaries screaming for failing red blood cells to pick up their game. The blue of impending death.

We've been called to a vegan restaurant called Tofu Fighters, and if the situation wasn't so desperate, Chad would be impetuously riffing, making all sorts of Dave Grohl-related jokes. A young employee was on his lunch break, scoffing down a lentil sandwich or lettuce pie or something equally bleak. Glass jars and porcelain mugs holding kale smoothies and carrot-cinos smashed on the sustainably sourced wooden floor as other servers ran to his aid after hearing a disturbance in the break room. They found their mate Dylan folded over, hands on knees. Something was wrong with him but he couldn't tell them what.

Even now, his wide eyes suggest a man looking into the void, but unable to scream at it. The void is looking and screaming back, though.

The half-eaten sandwich on the lunchroom table is a dead giveaway. This is a classic ambulance practice scenario come to life. A patient who can't breathe, and the only way to figure out why is to have impeccable situational awareness. Chad begs the kid to cough – to stimulate his body's built-in safety system that's designed to stop even the clumsiest of epicureans from inhaling their meals into the wrong hole and choking to death. All he gets is a terrified finger pointing into a mouth that no sound can come out of. No ability to speak, splutter, gag or retch.

I slip the infrared rubber probe of our oxygen saturation monitor onto one of the patient's fingers and realise that he's beyond coughing up this foreign object. It reads 60 per cent. And it's dropping. Fast. Something is lodged deep down there.

'Stuff it, time for back blows,' says Chad, realising the futility of the kid getting his lunch back up on his own. 'Come here, buddy.'

Chad drags Dylan towards him by his arm and spins him around. He opens the face of his right palm and fires five sharp jabs into the space between the kid's shoulder blades. Dylan offers a pained grunt with every connection of Chad's short strikes, but nothing dislodges or flings out of his gullet and splatters on the opposite wall like it would in a Monty Python skit.

Then Dylan collapses. Unconscious. There's no drama or the side-to-side swaying action of a dying swan. He just falls backwards. Chad catches him and lays him out on the floor.

'Aaagghhh. You've killed him,' squeals the restaurant manager.

Chad's no pipsqueak. And knowing his gym regime, and having seen the sting his back blows delivered, I almost think the same for a second. Then I glance at the oxygen meter again: 20 per cent.

'Settle down, mate,' says Chad. 'If anything's going to kill him, it's the chickpea that's blocking his windpipe. Now hand me the bloody laryngoscope, would you?'

Chad motions me towards our Oxyviva kit – arguably the most important bit of gear we carry besides the defibrillator. It's built for situations exactly like this, when we need to fix someone's airway. If you don't have an airway, you're dead. Simple as that. There's no point treating anything else if you can't fix the A in ABC. B for breathing is a little redundant if the hole for the breaths to go in is blocked.

I unzip the kit and pull out two silver implements: a thick handle about the size of a Berocca tube that uses two C-cell batteries to power a small LED light at the top of it, and a curved blade that's reminiscent of a toucan's beak. Snapping the two together activates the light, and the beam flows down the arc of the blade. Together, the pieces form a medieval instrument that looks, somewhat eerily, like a miniature Grim Reaper's scythe.

I toss the 'scope to Chad. He's already kneeling and assuming the airway position and manipulating Dylan's flaccid head so that the base of his skull tilts towards the ground, opening his mouth and optimising Chad's view down his throat. Chad slips the handle of the 'scope into his left hand so he's holding it like a ski-pole, with the blade at the bottom pointing upwards. His right hand cradles the crown of Dylan's floppy noggin as he slides the blade of the laryngoscope between the pair of cyanotic lips, into the right-hand corner of the mouth, so that he's able to scoop up Dylan's tongue and sweep it off to the left to visualise what's obstructing the airway. The bigger and chunkier patients that we're used to have big, chunky airway anatomy, making this a difficult process. Luckily for Chad, Dylan's edamame and flaxseed diet means his BMI is below average – a rare find in our industry – and he achieves the view he needs.

'Suction,' commands Chad.

Target acquired. Chad's got eyes on the blockage. I pass him the rubber suction hose with the diligence of a surgery assistant. He gets to work, feeding the rigid end of the suction hose into Dylan's mouth, parallel to the laryngoscope blade. Nothing comes up the tube.

'Shit!' he says. 'It's too thick. Forceps!'

I scurry back to the Oxyviva and grab the Magills – a pair of long, skinny tongs that bend at an obtuse angle to conform to the shape of the oropharynx so they can grasp whatever slippery little gremlin has lodged itself down there. I fling them over and Chad feeds them in.

'What the hell is this?' says Chad as he clamps up and down on the handles of the forceps, desperately grappling with the intruder that's stopping airflow from going in and out of Dylan's vocal cords. 'I can't get any purchase on it.'

'It's got to be something vegan. We're all vegans. We only employ vegans here. It's policy,' says the manager somewhere in the background.

'Righto mate, bit busy for the saving-the-world stuff right now. Maybe later when I'm done saving this bloke.' Chad's unflappable. 'Shit, this is the stiffest bit of tofu I've ever seen. It should be crumbling but it's just one big chunk.'

He continues the wrestle between forceps and foreign food invader. The blue tinge in Dylan's lips has now consumed his entire face. It's spread to his fingertips as well. The oxygen meter has stopped reading. Where there was a number, there's now just three blinking dashes. No one can remember when he last took a breath. I decide I'd better check for a pulse. I press two fingers to Dylan's neck.

'Got no carotid here, mate. I'm going to start CPR,' I tell Chad.

I kneel next to the body and ready myself for chest compressions.

'C'mon. C'mon,' says Chad, still fidgeting with the forceps.

He's willing the forceps to grip the obstruction. It's a ticking time bomb and there's only seconds to decide between snipping red or green. A bead of sweat drips from Chad's nose onto Dylan's lifeless face. It's gross. It's also the least of the patient's worries right now.

I interlock my fingers, form an upside-down triangle with my arms, and place the base of my right palm into Dylan's sternum. The bassline from 'Another One Bites the Dust' starts playing in my head.

'Gotcha, you bastard!' says Chad, whipping the forceps back with force.

Clinging to the end of the instrument, between the blades, is a fleshy, white, half-chewed clump of food about the size of a 50-cent piece. Chad holds it up proudly between the forceps. He's a fisherman who's just reeled in the greatest catch of his life. A new father who's just delivered his own baby.

We all stare at the chunk so intently we almost forget about Dylan. Then the noise of his body reanimating reminds us all to look down. Dylan coughs. Then he splutters. Then he starts to heave in great, thick mouthfuls of oxygen. Air is his body's oasis after it's been deprived in a desert of hypoxia. Warmth and colour return to his skin and his muscles regain tone. His revival comes a split second before I break all his ribs with CPR. After 10 seconds of a violent, forced reintroduction to the world of breathing, Dylan sits bolt upright. He continues to drag air into his lungs at a rapid rate, looking around the room, trying to figure out what all the commotion is about as his brain readjusts to the world.

'Almost got the *Best of You*, this one,' quips Chad.

Oh no, I think. Foo Fighters gags incoming.

Chad dangles the piece of food in front of Dylan, who still looks confused.

'It's *Times Like These* you've got to consider yourself lucky. You should buy a lotto ticket or perhaps even *Learn to Fly*.'

Chad's just pulled off a big save. And he knows it. So the jokes are flowing. But no one else has picked up on it yet.

'I think you might be a bit of a *Pretender*, though.'

Now everyone looks confused.

'You see, I know my chicken schnitties, been eating them *All My Life*, and this is no block of coagulated soy milk. No, mate, this is some grain-fed, lightly crumbed, mallet-pounded breast meat, my friend.'

Dylan starts going pale like he's choking again.

'So you might want to tell the boss here that you're not actually a vegan. Wouldn't want to keep him waiting *Everlong*.'

Chad drops the forceps on the break-room table like a hot mic, chicken chunk still in situ. Then he just walks out the door. Everyone looks at me. I just shrug at them.

'There goes *My Hero*,' I say.

Reprieve is short lived from the norm of triviality in the Bankstown area. For every Dylan who gets thrown a lifebuoy just seconds before he's swallowed by a final wave of doom, there's a thousand others that covet a

Thai cave rescue for themselves when all they need is a bandaid. I wonder if any of these people would call the fire department to blow out a candle when they know there could be housefires out there. It seems a worthy comparison.

The biggest positive is that Chad's getting endless new punters to play the fool for. In return, they're giving him a raft of farcical circumstances to work with and craft new gags from. It would be unfair not to share some notable moments from his highlight reel:

The woman outside the ED doors of Auburn hospital who wants us to take her back to her Surry Hills surgeon at 10pm because her new breast implants are hurting:

'How much did they cost?'

'About $20,000.'

'That's udderly ridiculous. Guess that's the price of inflation. It does bounce around a lot.'

The hoarder who gets pinned to the floor when a pile of his junk falls on him and is only saved from death by starvation when his wife returns from visiting her mother down the coast:

'I'm telling you I was just in the middle of cleaning all this up.'

'Save it for another time, buddy. And hang on to this one, love, he's a real keeper.'

The Indian man who tries to best his dad in a chilli-eating competition and calls an ambulance because he can't handle the pain of his burning arse:

'How heavy was this chilli pepper? We need to know.'

'How would I know that?'

'You'd give it a weigh, give it a weigh, give it a weigh now.'

Humour is what gets us through the nonsense. Once you realise what a joke most things on this job are, being a comedian is the only thing that makes sense. Chad's unlike ordinary paramedics who still believe we're all about helping people and making a difference. He's seen the true face of society and chosen to become a reflection of it, not fight it or pretend it doesn't exist. It's a state of Zen, a place of paramedic Nirvana that I want to join so I don't short circuit. Or go grey before I'm 30.

That said, we're craving a run of properly sick patients to smash the tedium. We can only play the fool for so long. We should be careful what we wish for. Because we get finally get it. And it's the job neither of us want.

The dispatcher tells us we have a Code 26. Chad's unfazed at first because he's forgotten what the rarely used number represents. I've got a better memory for the unusual.

'Ah fuck,' I say.

'What?'

'Code Twenty-Six, mate. Sexual assault.'

We're not equipped for this. There's no training manual or textbook explaining how to manage this one. There's no linear set of instructions like 1) attach defibrillator pads, 2) shock patient in cardiac arrest. We even ask the dispatcher if there are any female crews around, as they'd be more appropriate than two blokes. There isn't. It's just us.

Police are already inside the unit when we arrive. They're perplexed at seeing two men instead of at least one female paramedic. I mutter something about under-resourcing, being busy, *you know how it is*. Coherent sentences are difficult to form right now.

Chad offers to take one for the team and speak to the patient. I hang back and get a backstory from a female police officer. She tells me the offender climbed through the patient's window. Her boyfriend was asleep next to her. I look around the spartan apartment. There's only a couch and a coffee table in the open-plan living area and kitchen we're standing in. Two bedrooms and a bathroom branch off it. The once white floor tiles are a coarse beige from years of dust and neglect. The coffee table is over-spilling with bongs, used syringes, empty soft drink cans and unopened mail.

I hear Chad cringe internally in the bedroom when he hears himself ask the patient how she's feeling. He retreats back to us in the living room. He's got no answers. No solution. Nobody does. Chad can see there's nothing we can do in terms of life-saving interventions. It's not right to even approach the patient and take her blood pressure. He's asks me to grab a blanket from the van and he'll get the female police officer to escort the patient down and ride with her to hospital.

I head down the stairs and realise how high up we are. We're on the third storey of this unit block. I knew this when we first arrived because I was mildly puffed from lugging our gear up the stairs. It's an ongoing joke when we arrive at the top floor of lift-free apartment buildings for patients claiming to have breathing problems that turn out to be mild anxiety; we usually end up being more short of breath than they are.

'Wait. We're at least 10 metres off the ground here. How the hell did somebody climb through her bedroom window?' I say to the cops. 'I'm pretty sure these sorts of criminals aren't carrying ladders around.'

The cops nod in agreement. Good thing the detectives haven't arrived yet.

'And the part about her boyfriend being asleep next to her while it happened,' I continue. 'That seems very odd.'

More agreement. The female officer probes the patient discreetly. But that's all it takes.

It turns out the whole story was fabricated. An act of deception because the couple had run out of money to buy heroin and weed with. They'd heard Centrelink offers emergency payments to victims of sexual assault and planned on using it as a fraudulent loophole, no matter what depths they would have to sink to.

Chad's so despondent he can't even make a joke. I don't know whether to feel anger, sadness or revert to our faithful coping mechanism and clutch for a wisecrack myself. I consider it, but it doesn't feel appropriate. We sit in silence in the ambulance, beaten. PTSD is what finishes off most paramedics, not running out of banter. This is what they mean by the tears of a clown when there's no one around.

Most ambos just get by complaining to each other and hoping that by paying their monthly union fees some miracle will solve all our problems. But unions offer futile tactics for demanding better, such as writing messages on the sides of our trucks and refusing to enter patient's billing details in our medical records (nobody pays anyway!). The majority of paramedics see the idea of having different unions represent us, which usually results in them disagreeing with each other, as one of the biggest obstacles for change, only fuelling the indifference of aloof politicians.

Chad and I decide the only way to effect change is with mass public awareness and outrage. We just need the platform to disseminate it.

13

SCREENED OUT

'We want the real deal,' the reality TV producer tells me in a Skype meeting. 'We want your natural reactions. You can swear; you can cry. Make jokes. Don't do anything you wouldn't do if the cameras weren't there.'

She's promising big things: a new reality show focusing on paramedics. Though the idea is hardly new at all. Every few years, TV production companies dole out another fly-on-the-wall medical drama showing the daily struggles and harrowing trauma medics must deal with while maintaining their composure and treating patients with compassion and dignity. But this is going to be different, I'm assured: 000 calls are at record highs and no amount of media campaigns and advertising strategies is having an impact on bringing the volume down. However, an overseas version of this show has been linked to declining numbers of trivial calls, so our service has decided to entertain the idea of participating in a local edition. Now they just need talent.

Chad and I are the first to apply as soon as we see the email. If it's reality they want, we're the ones to bring it. Neither of us have a filter between our brains and our mouths when confronted with something outrageous. We won't be giving any sob stories about life-changing epiphanies that drew us to the profession as if it was our destiny. There'll be no utterings of *there, there* and *call us again anytime!* when nuisances ring us up to take out their bins or drive them to the chemist.

No, this is our chance to make a real change.

Chad and I want a platform to show the public the type of calls we spend most of our time going to in the south-west. *A Current Affair* may be able to expose dodgy builders and shonky kitchen appliances, but it can't lift the lid on people who waste the time of the emergency services because of something called patient confidentiality. But follow us two around with a cameraman and bunch of GoPros in the back of our rig and we won't hold back.

'Rest assured, nothing we film will be used against you, either,' says the producer. 'We're not looking for any *gotchas* if anyone slips up or makes mistakes.'

We're on.

Fast forward a month and Chad and I are sitting in a brand-new ambulance, kitted out with windscreen-mounted HD cameras and a shooter–producer with a shoulder rig riding in the back. The production company has eaten up our audition antics and decided to cast us. We're in just as much disbelief about this development as our paramedic colleagues are. Now we just need to make some cinematographic magic.

Our first patient is pleasant enough – a 70-year-old gent who's been hit by an acute burst of dizziness. Not exactly a pupil-dilating, sphincter-pinching traumatic misadventure, but he's more than accommodating to the cameras when Chad asks if it's okay if our shooter, Dan, comes in. We have friendly back-and-forth banter with the man about the Cronulla Sharks hat he's wearing and have a poke around his military memorabilia. It's the typical convivial yet uninspiring everyday ambulance visit that bulks out most of our days. Sure, our performance won't win us a Logie, but it's a feel-good interaction. The man's got a decent enough medical history, too, so we can't rule out his head spin isn't an underlying cardiac event, though it's most likely just some vertigo. We run him up to hospital for the usual gamut of tests that'll likely see him discharged before lunchtime.

We're going to need some juicier material than this to get our point across.

Then something even worse happens – a real emergency drops in. We're tasked to a cardiac arrest. Oh well, if we can't be pioneers of saving the ambulance service from an overburdened implosion, at least we might look like heroes.

Chad belts us along an arterial road and navigates through a maze of streets and avenues to find the self-contained retirement village we're after. An elderly lady guides us through to where her husband lays on the living room floor of the tiny flat. I cringe internally when Chad offers a very hurried query of consent for filming, because there's no time for small talk on this one. The lady appears to grant our wish but between our rushing and her bewilderment, she could have said anything. Dan the cameraman can have a better chat with her later.

One of the village staff nurses is performing chest compressions on the lady's husband but something looks off. I can see breathing so I ask the nurse to step aside briefly. I put two fingers where the man's carotid artery should be and feel a steady, bounding pulse. He's certainly not in cardiac arrest, but still severely unwell. All signs point to a sudden, massive haemorrhagic stroke.

'Oh look, they've gotten the IC out of bed,' says Chad in his deadpan manner as two of our senior colleagues walk through the front door.

He's referring to the widely held view that intensive care paramedics get left alone by our control centre, particularly on night shifts, and only have their sacred reclining time disturbed for the biggest emergencies, of which there are few. It's a highly coveted role that almost every paramedic aspires to – a new level that brings a huge variety of extra skills and medications to your arsenal, ones that can peel the direst patients out of their disastrous predicaments. But it's also a highly competitive unit, with course entry being notoriously difficult and seldom open for application. Only a small percentage of paramedics ever achieve the sought-after senior role.

Tamara and Stephen discreetly laugh off Chad's gag and help us carry out the man on a scoop board. Very little treatment can be offered by us at this point besides diesel therapy. A major blood vessel in the man's brain has burst and is leaking all over his intercranial cavity. The pressure shifts in the space send his blood pressure sky-high, paralysing him and reducing his level of consciousness to comatose. A neurovascular surgeon is the only person who can assist at this point and even then, given the man's age, their options will be limited. A 'big bleed' is usually terminal.

The wife rides up front during the transport and Chad's usual erratic whimsicality turns serious as she tries to pry information out of him from the passenger seat.

'Yes, he's still breathing, and his heart is still beating, darl.'

'No, he's not awake right now and he can't hear you.'

'Not sure exactly what's gone wrong, but it looks like a big stroke.'

'You'll need to ask the doctors that one.'

We arrive at hospital and wish the lady the pervasive *All the best!* as the hospital staff whisk her through the doors to the CT scanner room, her husband beside her on a hospital gurney, still inanimate and frozen. Cameraman Dan forgoes going back inside to ask her to sign the media consent form. We don't blame him. We know she'll soon be a widow. The last thing she needs is the memory of the last day with her husband syndicated eternally on TV.

Chad's got a theory that fibromyalgia is a made-up disease, that there's a global cabal of doctors who have gotten together, emerging from shadows in ritualistic ceremonies to conspire about how to deal with nuisance patients who complain that they're always in pain all over their bodies. Or patients who are always whinging they're tired and have no energy*. So as a collective they've come up with an esoteric name for a group of symptoms to appease patients that are never sated – patients who want a medical term they can display proudly like a badge of honour. It sounds like tinfoil-hat material, and would make a great monologue for TV, but every day I spend in the emergency world I become more inclined to agree with Chad's assertions.

Physical pain is a very specific, targeted phenomena. New age 'woke' definitions will declare that pain is not just associated with actual tissue damage anymore but can be an emotional experience caused by that which *resembles* tissue damage. These researchers mustn't have conducted their studies in the south-west, where pained emotional experiences are so pernicious that if we handed out morphine to every patient, we'd create an enclave of a million smackheads. The Afghan farmers who grow the

* See chronic fatigue.

opioid poppies for Big Pharma to synthesise wouldn't be able to replant their crops quickly enough, either.

One of the big mysteries modern sciences can't solve is how to create strong pain relief without side effects. So we need to be cautious when delivering powerful analgesia.

Sam is in the middle of a divorce; however, he's still living with his soon-to-be ex-wife. The call to his address is suitably vague, just stating that a 42-year-old male has severe pain. He's on his bed, writhing and groaning, oblivious to the cameraman hovering over my shoulder. I try to offer him a quick spiel about wanting to be filmed or not but am drowned out by his wailing. I attempt an assessment, but everything gets the same answer between anguished yelps.

'What's wrong?' I ask.

'My fibromyalgia.'

'Where does it hurt?'

'Owww. My fibromyalgia.'

'You'll need to be more specific,' I say.

'IT'S MY DAMN FIBROMYALGIA. WHAT IS IT YOU DON'T UNDERSTAND. Owww.'

Chad's had enough. He's already walked out of the bedroom. Sam's wife, Rita, tags along with him.

I decide I'm getting nowhere, so I reach for the medication kit and snap a tourniquet around Sam's left arm, which is dangling off the side of the bed. If he says he's in pain, he's in pain. Who am I to question or judge that?

'No, no. They can never get a vein. They usually give me the stuff up the nose.'

'Usually? How many ambulances are you calling?' I ask.

'A lot lately. It's been getting really bad.'

The 'stuff up the nose' he's referring to is intranasal fentanyl – a powerful anaesthetic that's 100 times more potent than morphine. We only use it in desperate situations where we can't gain intravenous access to administer pain relief; instead, it gets delivered into the nostrils by a spraying device that atomises the drug from a liquid into a fine mist, much like commonly used nose sprays for congestion from colds.

I shrug and unbuckle the tourniquet. I'm not going to persist with piercing his flesh at random intervals with a sharp metal stick. It'll just create the unnecessary potential for infection and I'm currently having a bad run with cannulas anyway, so fentanyl up the nose seems like the easiest, and safest, option. I draw the medication out of its sealed vial into the misting device and shoot it into Sam's nostrils in three short, alternating bursts. Relief floods over him instantly. As does silence over the room.

That worked remarkably quick.

'Off to hospital then?' I ask Sam, expecting little resistance.

He nods with a drowsy grin and springs from the bed like he's Grandpa Joe and I'm holding his golden ticket to the Chocolate Factory. He walks out of his room, down the hallway, and out to the ambulance, as if the excruciating pain he was crippled by less than a minute ago never happened.

I pack up the drug kit and head outside as well. Chad grabs my arm and pulls me aside in the front yard before I make it to the van. Sam's already set himself up on the stretcher, content and comfortable in his doped-up state.

'Mate, I think you've just been played by a seeker,' Chad says.

'Oh, I definitely have,' I say. 'But what can you do?'

'Make good TV, that's what. Rita's just been telling me how all this carry-on only started when she put in for a divorce. He's calling ambulances and going to hospital all the time. All the doctors keep telling him there's nothing wrong, but he keeps insisting he's suddenly got pain everywhere all the time. Poor woman is at her wits' end. My bloody fibromyalgia theory is right.'

He gives me a triumphant backhanded smack on the shoulder.

'I've just realised I've been here before,' chimes in cameraman Dan. 'Yeah, a few weeks ago with the other Bankstown crew.'

'Who was it?' asks Chad.

'Will and Taylor.'

'I've got Taylor's number. I'll call her.'

Over the phone, Taylor tells Chad she's been to Sam several times now, once with cameraman Dan. She's expressed concerns to him about his opioid-seeking behaviour and the potential long-term side effects on his health. Sam didn't want to hear it so she relayed those concerns to the hospital. However, putting plans in place to stop overuse of pain medication is a soldier of time that marches slowly. For the foreseeable future, Sam will be allowed to call ambulances and request pain relief as much as he wants. Various crews have attended to him, according to Taylor, some giving analgesia, some not. He's known to keep calling until he gets a crew that gives him what he wants.

'Did you see all the boxes of OxyContin in his room, all prescribed by different doctors?' Taylor says over speaker.

Sam's spiralling into a dangerous predicament – and when he calls for help, we're the ones who find ourselves in just as difficult a situation. We don't want to deny someone pain relief if they say they're in agony; it's not our place to judge patients or deny them potential comfort. On the other hand, we don't want to be enablers and send someone down a pathway of addiction and long-term damage, both physical and mental.

'Bro, this could be the redemption story of the year. They can show Taylor's footage, then show you a few weeks later having a heart-to-heart and convincing him to get clean.'

I climb into the back of the ambulance with Sam, better informed but no less confused about how to best aid his plight. Busted bones and nasty wounds I know how to mend. But I never took the class on tormented souls.

'You guys are heroes. You know that, right?' Sam says as I clamber into the treatment seat.

Must be the generous dose of Fentanyl talking.

'Oh, thanks mate. Hey, you mind saying that once for the camera?' I laugh, pointing to a GoPro mounted in the cabin.

'Oh, I'm going to be on TV? Sweet! Yeah, you guys are awesome.'

'Cheers, Sam. Now let's talk about all this Fentanyl you've been having . . .'

Cameraman Dan follows us for the next three weeks. The footage he gets is typically matter-of-course: chest pains, elderly falls, minor wounds, faints, diabetic problems. Not exactly edge-of-the-seat, white-knuckle stuff. Just a fair representation of the banality that is daily paramedic life. Between cases, Dan films our musings about other services patients can use or how it's just as appropriate for family members to transport ill relatives to hospital when the only piece of equipment of ours they use is the back seat in the ambulance. Hopefully our conversations can be spliced in between other crews performing life-saving heroics on people squashed by machinery and getting flung off their motorbikes.

The show finally airs. We watch the first episode. It's we what expect – the ubiquitous medical cliches sneak in, a smattering of heroics make an appearance, data about how busy we are gets a mention. Chad and I don't feature, however. Maybe next week, we think. Next week comes. We don't make the edit. Neither do our quips and philosophies show up in episodes three, four or five – all the way through to the series finale. We've been benched, dropped from the squad, jersey-less.

Did we swear too much? Too many controversial conversations? Faces only good for radio?

Chad calls one of the show's liaisons whose contact number he finds on an old email from the production company. Consent – that was the hurdle that couldn't be jumped, he's told. Hardly any patients filmed in our presence were interested in being on camera – some understandably wanting to keep their medical issues private, some likely wanting to avoid public shame and contempt for their life choices. Turns out Sam must have changed his mind. And without any footage of treating patients, the ramblings of two random ambos in the front of their van would look out of place, no matter how much flashy editing and dramatic music was put to it. It's an issue that plagued the entire production, apparently, but enough footage managed to be knocked together to make a series – just none of it featured us because the south-west citizens are particularly tentative. Our dream of single-handedly being the golden saviours of the service, paraded around in shoulder-borne litters like ancient Egyptian kings, dies with that phone call. A legacy isn't always something you get to choose.

But the dream of reducing our own laborious work-load doesn't perish in that moment. Just days after the show has come off air, Chad's work inbox is still open, and I see a new email that's just landed, highlighted in bold.

It's something else we can sign up for. Something to engender change and, at the very least, buy us a few hours' sleep and take some of the sting out of our relentless night shifts: intensive care paramedic applications have just opened.

14

GIVEN THE SHAFT

All paramedics wear a distinctly coloured badge and set of epaulettes on their shoulders. These mean nothing to the public – we're all just ambulance drivers. Instead, the differently shaded patches of fabric allow us to distinguish each other's rank, or clinical level, among ourselves. This is particularly useful when working in unfamiliar areas and encountering crews we don't regularly mingle with, so that during a high-stress, chaotic incident, such as a major motor-vehicle accident or multi-patient situation, we can quickly identify which paramedics can and can't perform certain skills and how best to distribute the workload.

Intensive care paramedics sit at the top of the food chain and wear the coveted 'gold on the shoulders' – a pair of epaulettes daubed with yellow writing that signals not just higher rank and seniority, but a wealth of know-how and experience from years of grinding on the road and covering all manner of high-octane emergencies. The emblems also communicate that the person wearing them survived the notoriously horrendous ICP course, a training program whispered about in hushed voices with the same mystic reverence as Navy SEAL bootcamp. It's said that the lectures and classwork on advanced anatomy, physiology, pharmacology and clinical skills are relentlessly intense, and this knowledge is then expected to be regurgitated verbatim at a moment's notice so that future ICPs can treat only the highest acuity emergencies with military precision. The course is meant to break wills and destroy dreams and is survivable by only the most resilient. And those who make it through are handsomely and fairly rewarded with the pinnacle of paramedic compensation: sleep on night shift.

Chad and I apply for the course on a whim, barely meeting the minimum length-of-service requirement to even be eligible. Half-joking, half as practice for a proper crack in a few years' time, we figure it can't hurt to see what the process is like. Knowing we're competing with most of the ambulance service, all of whom are more experienced than us, we fill out the few extended-response questions on the email application then promptly forget about it and move on with our lives. Within a couple of weeks, we're both shocked to receive an invite to take part in the next stage of testing: a multiple-choice test to be held at Ambulance HQ.

'Maybe everybody gets through to this stage and the email application is just a formality,' I offer to Chad.

We attend the quiz day and take our seats at computers in a group of 20 or so other paramedics, spread apart and invigilated by a senior educator to prevent any chicanery. It feels like being back in high school, but cheating at this point would only be cheating yourself – the rumour is that 250 ambos have applied to become ICPs and there's only 12 spots in the upcoming class.

Chad and I leave the room, both shaking our heads. Anatomical and biological questions cropped up in topics we haven't thought about since our paramedic uni degrees, and once outside we're immediately googling on our phones to see if there's any hope our guesses were right.

'Oh well, we never really planned on getting in anyway,' says Chad. 'At least we know to study harder next year.'

It's disappointing. A small part of me hoped I'd fluke my way in and make an early ascension to the heights of intensive care paramedic to escape the monotony of being a general duties paramedic in Bankstown. I resign myself to at least another year of this and immediately return to the grind of nursing-home transfers, old folks falling over and busting their hips, and weird blokes getting foreign objects lodged in their butts (*I swear I just fell over and it was there!*).

A few more weeks pass and then my inbox pings again. It's another invite back to Ambulance HQ, this time for an interview and practical scenario, the final stage of selection. Chad gets the same email.

I might actually have a chance here, I think to myself.

A random paramedic I've never met before eyes me suspiciously as we both sit outside the interview room waiting to be called in. We don't say anything to each other and quickly avert our gaze every time a hint of eye contact is almost made. Another senior educator emerges from behind the door. He makes us flip a coin. The winner gets to choose whether they want to go into the room for the interview first or head off elsewhere to attempt the practical scenario. I win the toss and choose the scenario. I figure there's more chance of bombing the interview, so if I do that first and flop I'll be totally demoralised and put no effort into the scenario. Interview questions I've got no control over, whereas in a medical simulation I'm just doing my job, albeit on a mannequin. It should be straightforward enough. That's my logic, anyway.

Turns out it is completely straightforward. It's me who overcomplicates the situation in my head. I'm told by the educator running the scenario that I've been called to a restaurant for a young male with breathing problems. This immediately transports me back to when Chad and I saved Dylan's life at Tofu Fighters and I think I've got this in the bag. But I start to get strange looks from the examiners and they say I'm getting no response from the patient when I start treating him as though he's choking. I'm asking him to cough and readying myself to start striking him between the shoulder blades. His breathing is only getting worse, I'm informed.

Shit, I'm fucking this right up.

Cold puddles of sweat form in my armpits and I feel sick.

Why am I so invested in this? I never even expected to get past the first phase.

Instead of increasing my panic, this thought is exactly what I need to relax. I have a moment of clarity.

'Wait, what kind of restaurant is this?' I ask the examiner, who's acting as the voice of the plastic dummy patient that's sitting up on a chair.

'Thai restaurant,' he says cheerfully.

'And what were you eating?'

'Pad Thai. What else?'

'And are you allergic to anything?' I ask, but I already know the answer.

'Yeah, peanuts.'

Jackpot.

I start jabbing the patient (mannequin) in the meaty bit of his thigh with shots of intramuscular adrenaline and pop a salbutamol nebuliser on for his wheezy airway. He starts to improve. His breathing eases and oxygen levels are rising. I slide an IV cannula into a plastic vein that's got a pilot hole already pre-drilled from a million practice attempts from trainee paramedics and other ICP hopefuls who have used this dummy before me.

I hang a bag of IV fluid and am about to connect it when the patient suddenly stops breathing. The ECG monitor stops beeping and the regular intervals of thin triangles on the screen flatten out to a single, unbroken line. The patient's just gone into cardiac arrest. And I couldn't be happier. Everyone knows to always expect the patient to go into arrest in a scenario and I've prepared for this moment. I finish the remaining minutes of the simulation ventilating, compressing and defibrillating at the appropriates moments until the examiner calls time. I leave the room feeling chuffed with myself. I just hope I didn't spend too long bumbling around with my choking misdiagnosis at the beginning and delay giving the life-saving adrenaline beyond what the examiners might consider an acceptable time.

I head back to the interview room for the second phase. As soon as it starts, I know it's over. I bomb. Hard. I've spent all my time studying for questions about complicated medication doses and wild situations where I'm required to manage 50 patients in a plane crash or terrorist attack, but this barely crops up. I've totally neglected to think about questions on leadership, peer support, teaching and ethics. These are all important characteristics of an intensive care paramedic, just not the ones everyone immediately thinks of, and form the focus of the interview. I resort to the only tactic I know to dig myself out of these situations: bullshitting. It's a tried-and-tested formula used by generations of young men to worm out of all manner of situations, ranging from meetings with the school principal to inquisitions by girlfriends. I imagine Chad in an identical room somewhere else doing the same, stuttering through questions he's got absolutely no clue how to answer but somehow coming across sincerely with his weaponised hyperactivity charm. It won't ace the interview for us but it might get a couple of sympathy points so we don't come across to senior staff members in our education department as incompetent imposters that have somehow been given paramedic uniforms. I answer the final question and the panel tells me there's still 10 minutes left. They ask if I'd like to revisit any questions and add to my answers. I'm mentally defeated and have already checked out and accepted my fate, so I just tell them no.

MY OFFICE. THIS AFTERNOON.

Weeks later, Chad is cc'd into the same email from our station manager, Ivan.

It only takes these four words to know we've fucked up. There's no other reason for this tone of email when it's sent to the both of us. I'm just trying to think what dodgy act we've been caught out in that has made Ivan so angry.

You think this is about when I pulled into that disabled spot to buy lunch?

Chad's text tells me he's seen the email as well.

Could be, I reply. *Maybe someone took a photo and sent in a complaint.*

I was only there 30 seconds! says Chad.

Chad and I meet outside Ivan's office.

'Shut the door,' says Ivan.

We shuffle into his office, making sure to look remorseful.

'Sir, I swear, it was three in the afternoon,' says Chad. 'We hadn't eaten since breakfast. I'd forgotten to bring lunch. It was only 30 seconds, I swear. Alright, a minute, max.'

'Chad, what the hell are you talking about?' says Ivan.

'Parking in the disabled space. Wait . . . this isn't about that?

'Disabled space? What are you . . . actually, forget it. I don't even want to know about that right now. We'll come back to it. No, I want to talk about something far more serious.'

Oh shit. We've really fucked up.

'Sir, whatever it was . . .'

'Chad, just shut up for one minute of your life, would you?'

'Okay, sir. Sorry, sir.'

'Good. Thank you. Now, have either of you ever heard of Steven Bradbury?'

'The ice skater?' Chad asks, confused.

He hasn't made the connection yet. But I've just pieced together that this is Ivan's version of a Chad-esque stitch-up to break us some good news.

'No way,' I say.

'Yep,' says Ivan, knowing I've understood the reference. 'I got the call this morning. They're letting you two clowns into the intensive care course.'

The biggest shock about the course isn't that it's some kind of medical military bootcamp – it's the amount of endless, relentless PowerPoint presentations. I feel like I'm at university again, but instead of three years, we're expected to cram a whole degree's worth of knowledge into six weeks. And then there's the practice scenarios for the myriad new patient presentations we can now treat with our new drugs and skills: atropine for bradycardias*, amiodarone for tachycardias**, ketamine for severe pain, needle decompression for tension pneumothorax***, intubation and intragastric tubes to name a few. This sounds simple enough, but this is intensive care for a reason: all these patients are actively and very quickly trying to die. And their family members are screaming at us to save them. So are the junior paramedics. And the police. And the firefighters. It's like being thrown a hose and told to put out a house fire. Except the hose is a garden hose. And you aren't trained to put out a fire. And there's no water. The course gives

* Dangerously slow heart rates.

** Dangerously fast heart rates.

*** Collapsed lung. Usually found in victims who've been stabbed or shot in the chest. Ergo, needle decompression is a useful tool in areas where knives and guns are the weapons *du jour* – like south-west Sydney.

me a newfound respect for those who study medicine to become doctors.

There's also only time to show us each of these scenarios once due to the time consumed by the PowerPoints. Any more practice is to be done in our own time. We stay back for hours and hours each evening to get more simulation time well after our paid hours have ended. This puts a strain on my relationship back at home. My partner wants to know why I can't leave the textbooks alone for 30 minutes to go out for dinner or spend time with her. Then I start to wonder the same.

Why is this course stressing me out so much? I've done two uni degrees. Study is nothing foreign to me. And I joined this job thinking I'd be okay at it because I fancy myself as being able to stay calm under pressure more than the average person. I soon realise the cause of the worry. It's not the workload at all. It's the shame that returning to my old station will bring upon me if I fail the course. Failures don't happen very often because most people work hard and earn their place. But in my mind, I'm still an imposter, still junior and inexperienced, and flunking will validate this not just to me, but to everyone else who tried out and didn't succeed.

But after six weeks, countless exams, high-pressure tests with doctors watching on, snaps and meltdowns in front of the missus, somehow I make it through. So does everyone else on the course. We celebrate on the night of our final exam in the only appropriate way: with a river of beer and a guest appearance by a prosthetic penis that someone has 'borrowed' from one of the simulation mannequins. It's hardly the SAS capturing an artificial limb from a dead Taliban fighter – it seems the best souvenir us rookie ICPs can acquire is a veiny, four-inch rubber cock*.

The next morning, through headaches and hangovers, our course conveners give us the assignments for the stations where we'll be completing the on-road component of our intensive care training, and then working for permanently. Some people are staying put at their home stations, but most of us are moving again. Chad is off to work in the city somewhere. But the pounding ache in my temples is about to get more severe. And constant. I'm going to the only place worse than Bankstown: Liverpool.

* The penis was eventually returned to its rightful owner.

15
A CHANGE OF PACE

'You're going to see a lot more people die,' says Wendy. The same person who was my backup on the first cardiac arrest I attended is going to be my intensive care training officer. It's an ominous warning, but it's what I'm signing up for. Praying for storms doesn't always bring peace.

Intensive care ambulances are automatically assigned to every cardiac arrest call and, while not all of the calls are legitimate, the ones that are usually result in the most senior paramedic ending resuscitation in the patient's home and breaking the bad news to the family. Wendy should know; she's been doing it for more than 20 years. And those 20 years have given her sound judgement of what sort of person has the stones to handle the added pressure it takes to be an intensive care paramedic. We've always been on amicable terms, but now Wendy is the gatekeeper of my ICP badge, and she's not going to be easy to pass. Being friendly doesn't mean she's going to mollycoddle me, when one day I could be the one intubating a family member of hers.

Wendy's maleficent prophecy turns out, of course, to be true. As we begin navigating the higher-grade emergencies of the Liverpool area, death stalks me like an obnoxious motorist tailgating an ambulance to bypass traffic. From accidental overdoses in the heroin havens of Warwick Farm and Cabramatta, to the grandfather who hangs himself from a ratchet strap in his garage just days after his wife of 70 years passes away, it seems that at least twice a day I'm giving my 'spiel'. It's a rehearsed, formulaic script recited to family members which ticks all the essential points without being patronising or offering false hope.

'We put in a breathing tube and gave medications to get his heart going again but there was no response.'

'No, we can't use the defibrillator; their heart is past that point.'

'More CPR or taking her to hospital isn't going to change anything. I'm sorry, but she's died.'

It's blunt, honest and true. And it's the part of being a senior paramedic that classroom scenarios and PowerPoint presentations don't prepare you for. The tangible skills and rote-learned medication doses stored in my hippocampus are there to be dug out in high-stress situations. But once there are no more procedures to perform or medications to give and a patient is declared dead, there's no remote part of my brain from where I can produce comforting lines to make everything alright. There are only the dark recesses where more trauma is stored. But it's the logical left hemisphere that earns me my first save.

There's a cardiac arrest in a unit on a street we've nicknamed Black Tar Boulevarde, firstly because of the amount of heroin ODs crews have attended there over the years, and secondly because of its worn-out, council flat aesthetic and inhabitants whom Wendy calls 'cockroaches'; people who live in filth, ingest god knows what substances into their bodies, and never, ever die. Despite their best efforts.

The first crew is hard at work pumping the patient's chest. He's a stringy mid-40s male, but has that weathered look that adds 25 years in the awful way that only a lifetime of intravenous opioid abuse can do. The crew is delivering oxygen to him via the bag mask but it's not enough. Strangely, with heroin, it isn't the drug itself that kills the user, but the resulting respiratory depression that leads to apnoea*. With assisted ventilation, someone can have all the heroin in the world in their system and be totally fine – as long as someone (or something, i.e. a ventilator) is doing the breathing for them until the drug is cleared. So this is the perfect opportunity for an attempt at intubation – one of my newly acquired skills

* The cessation of breathing.

that involves threading a thin plastic tube in between a patient's vocal cords and into their lungs with the assistance of a laryngoscope. It's what anaesthetists do to keep you alive during surgery (and thus bill you a fortune so they can drive Porsches), but for paramedics it's a little more chaotic.

There's no clean, sterile environment where an assistant nurse hands us a bunch of pre-assembled tools and breathing circuitry on command. We need to unpack all the gear ourselves from a little yellow bag, then set it up as cleanly as possible on the carpet of a commission unit that's never seen a vacuum and has so much cigarette ash on it that it could be diagnosed with emphysema. Then we need to slide the tube into a tiny hole that's around a corner in the patient's throat while someone is doing hard compressions on their chest, making their airway bounce up and down. Add into that the sweat fogging up my goggles and the patient's drug buddy screaming in the background, and it becomes a bit like one of those old electric buzz wire games. Except the stakes are now elevated to those of Russian roulette, and if your fine motor skills aren't up to scratch, you don't just receive a mild electric shock and go back to the start; when the trigger gets pulled and you lose, someone dies.

Thankfully, with a bit of tweaking and manipulation, the tube glides into the hole it's supposed to (the one that's not the oesophagus; oxygen in the stomach doesn't do much good) and after another round of CPR the patient's heartbeat returns. Not only that, but the mastication of his lips around the plastic tube indicates that he's starting to wake up. It's unbelievable. Nobody ever comes back from pulselessness when I'm around. Especially not patients who have made these sorts of lifestyle choices. His pending resurrection might seem like a good thing, but we'd prefer him to stay asleep for now. His hypoxic brain and CPR-battered chest mean he won't be the happiest chap when he awakens, and probably won't be willing to walk down six flights of stairs and into the ambulance to spend a few days in the ICU. He'll just be an angry, confused, semi-conscious body that will only be a hazard to our safety, so I draw up a mixture of morphine and midazolam to keep him unconscious. Giving more opioids to an addict seems counterintuitive, but it's the best thing we can do for everyone involved.

'Might have a bit of trouble with that,' says Wendy, waving a small orange canister at me.

It's a Narcan nasal spray device, a small pump that contains the drug Naloxone, which reverses the effects of heroin. They've been becoming increasingly popular among heroin users due to their ease of use when someone accidentally ODs, and in turn result in fewer ambulance callouts and hospital admissions as well. Unfortunately, nasal spray medications require active circulation in the body to work, so when they're given after the point of cardiac arrest they tend to do little besides sit in the nostrils, instead of travelling through the blood vessels, which requires an active heartbeat. However, we've now restored the patient's circulation, so the Naloxone has been unleashed with force and is swimming with bad intentions through the patient's bloodstream, kicking little gremlins of China White in the opioid receptors of his nervous system. And it will do exactly the same to my morphine mixture that I want to use to keep our patient asleep.

As I'm considering all of this and thinking what my next move is going to be – because moments like this are how Wendy is judging whether I'm worthy of being an ICP – the patient makes a bunch of gagging noises. Then his right hand comes up and starts tugging on the breathing tube that's hanging out of his mouth. His reanimating corpse wants to pull out this strange object that's tickling his uvula. Instinctively I reach down and use a syringe to deflate air out of the spherical cuff that's holding the tube in place on the other side of his vocal cords so he doesn't rip them out. Then the tube comes out like a magician producing a coloured handkerchief out of his throat. The patient sits bolt upright. His face is full of life and colour. Twenty seconds ago, he was cold, pale and dead*.

---

* One thing Hollywood movies still haven't gotten right, even with all the advances in modern technology and CGI, is the pale blue and then ghostly white colour people turn when their heart stops. Often this starts happening well before the point of cardiac arrest, depending on the patient's condition. Out of either laziness or lack of research, directors seem to think we're supposed to believe someone has just died because they suddenly close their eyes and don't open them again, even though their face is still as warm and pink as the day they were born. It's a bit like the scenes where someone is in an induced coma but aren't connected to a ventilator so they can actually breathe.

'Fuck, not again,' says Dion.

He starts to stand up.

'Woah, woah, sit back down,' say four paramedics collectively.

His body has just suffered a cardiac arrest, one of the worst things it can endure. Exerting energy is the worst possible idea right now. And we don't really want to run the whole cardiac-arrest drill from the beginning again. Dion sits down.

'Shit, my chest hurts,' he says. 'You guys did CPR on me, didn't you?'

We all nod.

'Fark. Why does this keep happening?' he sighs.

'Not your first rodeo?' asks Wendy.

'Third time this week,' says Dion. 'Just give me a minute and I'll come with you to hospital.'

'Three times this week?' says Wendy. 'I think they must be sprinkling Fentanyl in your gear, pal. This is probably a sign it's time to give up.'

'Nah, they can't kill me,' he says with a toothy smile. 'I'm a cockroach.'

After dropping Dion off, my training continues. 'Good work with that tube,' says Wendy. 'We might make an ICP out of you yet.'

'Thanks,' I say. 'It wasn't the easiest one, and I feel like I need to shower after kneeling down in that place. Or at least change my pants.'

'Yeah, me too. Let's go back to station.'

'Got a pacemaker problem for you guys if you're ready.'

The dispatcher's voice comes through the radio with its usual impeccable timing.

'No worries, send it down,' replies Wendy. 'Hey, this could be your first chance to use ami or atropine.'

Ami, or amiodarone, is another of my newly acquired medications and is a powerful antiarrhythmic that's used to stop a deadly heart rhythm called ventricular tachycardia (VT). VT is one of the two shockable rhythms when a patient is in cardiac arrest. And it's even scarier when a patient suffering from it is conscious because they're unlikely to be that way for long unless something is done quickly. When the notes that drop down onto our data screen say *pacemaker not working*, this seems even more a possibility. A lot of modern pacemakers are also combined with internal cardiac defibrillators for patients who are prone to going into dangerous rhythms, so the fact that this one isn't working spells danger. The other possibility is that the pacemaker is no longer 'keeping pace' and the patient's heart is now beating dangerously slow. This is what my drug atropine will temporarily fix until we can get the patient to hospital where hopefully there's someone clever enough to fix a mechanical issue with a pacemaker.

'Wonder how they know it's not working?' says Wendy. 'Maybe it shocked them once but they can still feel their heart going 200 beats a minute.'

'Or maybe it keeps shocking them and won't stop,' I offer.

'Gee, that would suck.'

Wendy skirts through traffic like our ambulance is Mike Tyson slipping and weaving around the thundering hands of Lennox Lewis. Her years of experience driving lights and sirens in south-west Sydney traffic have developed into a speedy efficiency that's urgent without putting commuters at risk. The address we're heading to is well out of central Liverpool, in one of the new, swelling outer-suburban developments where residents take out million-dollar loans for a three-bedroom house with a black-tiled roof that's identical to 5,000 others on the same estate, all on 300 square metres with no backyard, no trees and touching gutters with the place next door. The Australian dream.

We knock on the front door.

'It's open,' squeaks a modest female voice.

I push the door open and am greeted with the worst sight I've seen in my career. A woman of about fifty years is lying in an ocean of shit in the hallway. Not shit as in hoarder junk. Actual human faeces.

'Oh god, I'm out,' says Wendy.

She gags and heads back to the ambulance, trying not to vomit.

'You sort this out and you can have the damn ICP badge today,' she calls out.

Every paramedic has their own personal kryptonite. For some it's vomit, others it's the simple phrase of being called an ambulance driver instead of a paramedic that sets them off. I've just discovered Wendy's. I can't fault her right now, though. This hallway is more squalid than the escape tunnel that Andy Dufresne used to crawl out of Shawshank State Penitentiary.

I can't see any safe way to approach the patient without getting my boots covered in excrement, so I just call out to the poor, marooned lady.

'I thought you were having a pacemaker problem?' I say.

'I am, love,' she replies. 'It's just . . . my pacemaker isn't in my chest like normal ones.'

'Where is it?'

'In my anus.'

'An *anal* pacemaker?'

'Yes, darling. It's constantly running so I'm not incontinent. I had a baby later in life and had been having problems with bowel control. The pacemaker uses electrical waves to stimulate the muscles, just like a heart pacemaker. Only instead of keeping my heart going, this one stops me pooping myself.'

'Right. I can see how it's not working then. How is there so much of this?'

'Well, because it's always going, sometimes I forget to turn it off for a few days and actually use the toilet. I was on my way down the hall to do it when I guess the battery must have died.'

'Okay, fair enough. Give me a minute and I'll figure something out.'

I retreat to the ambulance, where I find Wendy with the side door open, sitting on the step and looking green in the face, trying to gulp in fresh air.

'I think we need to call another crew to assist with this one,' I tell her.

'Rule number one of being an intensive care paramedic. Delegate to subordinates. Congratulations, you're now an ICP.'

She peels the Velcro-backed ICP badge off the left side of her shirt and flings it at me. Just metres from the world's greatest bowel motion, the torch has now been passed as well.

16

OF ICE AND MEN

The phone rings at 6.40pm, five minutes before we officially begin our shift. I've just stumbled through the station door and dispatch is already asking if the IC is ready to go: there's been a rollover on the M5 and the day-shift general duties crew will need backup. A trainee who's answered the phone is far too excited telling me this – to them it could be the biggest job of all time, but to me a rollover doesn't raise my pulse one beat anymore. I've never been to one where the occupants haven't self-extricated and been completely unharmed. Modern cars are far too safe. Which is a good thing for everyone, except rookie paramedics wanting to cut their teeth on major road trauma.

I haven't had time to use the bathroom, put down my bag or even find the keys to the van I'll be using tonight. I grunt at the probationer that I'll get the medications

I need and find an ambulance so we can head to the job. My partner, Mark, walks in and I tell him the good news. He's equally unimpressed. There's no omen for a bad night like being given work before you've even started work.

Mark grabs a set of keys and takes our bags to an ambulance. I head to the drug room and scribble a bunch of signatures in books to sign out our most potent medications – morphine, midazolam, fentanyl, methoxyflurane and ketamine – which are kept locked in safes. On the off chance this rollover victim has any injuries, they may well need one or two of these drugs. If they're really unlucky, they'll need them all. As much as the control centre wants us jetting to the scene like a rat running from a tidal wave, making their dispatch-time numbers look good, if we leave without medications we may as well be taking an Uber.

Mark's got the engine running and I slide into the passenger seat. We hurtle back the way I've just come, this time eastbound down the M5 carriageway.

'Didn't cause this one on your way in, did you?' laughs Mark.

'Mate, I'm not in that much of a hurry to get to night shift,' I say.

We fling under the Henry Lawson Drive overpass and a sudden drop-off in traffic on the opposite side of the road indicates the scene will be just up ahead – and that we'll need to turn around at the next off-ramp because the M5 is separated up the middle by a solid concrete barricade. Consequently, we'll also have to fight our way through both the congestion and the hordes of sticky-beaks looking for some excitement.

'There it is,' says Mark, pointing to the grassy verge that cambers upwards off the shoulder of the M5 East's lefthand lane.

A white van has left the road and, as expected, is the wrong way up. It's also facing the direction of oncoming traffic. Its roof is crumbled inwards like tinfoil. Below it, there's carnage on the asphalt. Police are frantically trying to slow and corral the passing motorists. Firefighters are hauling hydraulic tools out of their trucks, ready to cut and slice metal and free any trapped occupants from several other vehicles caught in the destruction.

We swing around at the River Road overpass and head back west, pushing through the rubberneckers. We use the shoulder but it's still slow. It's a tight squeeze between the Armco and the freight trucks in the left lane and the paperwork from losing a door mirror isn't worth saving a few seconds over.

We tuck in behind a police car that's stopped in the middle of the chaos, and a panting cop approaches my window as I'm zipping up my high-vis vest.

'The van driver is alright, but the worst is the passenger in that car over there,' she says, pointing to a hatchback that's missing most of its front end on the left side. 'He smashed her head on.'

'Head on?' I say, as I pull our kits out of the side door.

How do two vehicles travelling in the same direction have a head-on collision?

'Yeah, fuckin' dickhead off his face on ice driving the wrong way down the motorway,' says the officer. 'He walked away without a scratch. Don't worry about him; we've already got him in the cage truck.'

'Junkies always bounce,' laments Mark as he rounds the front of the ambulance to join me. 'Same as drunk drivers. They're so relaxed their bodies just turn to rubber in prangs.'

Ice. Meth. The crystal pistol. Having a glass barbeque. Whatever you want to call it. Nothing good has ever come from it except Grinspoon's music.

We make our way over to the totalled hatchback and see an unmistakable spiderweb pattern on the passenger side of the windscreen, indicating the glass has come into contact with a high-velocity, unrestrained human head. It's known as a 'bullseye', and while being the best advertisement there is for seatbelts, I've seen this type of impact turn solid scalps into half-empty goon bags. Without doubt, it means this patient is getting the works; they're going to have a high-mechanism head injury so they're going to need spinal precautions, a pelvic binder*, limb splinting and drugs. Lots of drugs.

---

* A belt that wraps around a patient's hips to close a fractured, or potentially fractured, pelvis to stop them from bleeding to death. Trust me when I say you're better off being stabbed than having an open-book pelvic fracture. It's exactly what it sounds like: the pelvis splays open like pages of a book causing the snapped bones to form hundreds of razor-sharp daggers that can't wait to sever all the major blood vessels that live in the pelvis at the smallest hint of movement.

The day-shift general duties crew is hard at work treating the patient. Mark leaves me with them so he can scout out anyone else who needs help and put out a radio report for more crews if needed.

Melanie, the patient, is in a bad way. I can tell instantly because every muscle in her body is tense and tight. She's fighting against the fireman in the backseat of the car who's trying to keep her neck in alignment. Her teeth are gritted, her eyes are wide and white and forked with red veins. She's groaning in a rhythmic, pained manner. Wet vermicelli noodles that were once unfractured arms try to lash out at the paramedics assisting her through the door she's trapped by. She's displaying all the tell-tale signs of a combative head injury. Part of Melanie's skull has been cracked, likely the part that smacked into the reinforced glass of the windshield. Fluid is leaking and shifting around her brain, putting pressure on different cerebral centres that control thoughts, emotions, breathing and other necessary functions of living. It's what's making her behave as though she's demonically possessed. Melanie looks like someone who ordinarily wouldn't complain if a restaurant brought out the wrong order.

A sudden wrong twist and any unstable fractures in her neck could slice into her spinal cord and paralyse her permanently. She needs a neurosurgeon immediately. Next best thing is an induced coma until she can make it to surgery. We're not trusted to perform those, but what we can do is give her a weapons-grade dose of ketamine, which will not only completely remove the immense pain that's sending her sympathetic nervous system into overdrive, it'll put Melanie into a catatonic state where her mind will gently float off to another realm. It's the most useful medication we carry as intensive care paramedics and when I regularly see the somnambulistic trance it puts people in, I can't fathom why anyone would do this stuff recreationally.

I inject the medication through an IV cannula my colleagues have managed to wrestle into Melanie's forearm, and it takes less than a minute to kick in. Her hyper-agitated state is now placid and dreamy but might only be that way for a small window. Ketamine is an unpredictable drug and can wear off just as rapidly as it comes on. We let the firefighters take over with their noisy toys and start the process of freeing Melanie from her mangled, automotive prison.

Creak, creak, creak, crunch. Creak, creak, creak, crunch.

The metal of the door frame twists and bends under the strain of the power tools and eventually pops off. We slide Melanie's limp body out of the seat on a backboard and load her onto the stretcher where we can snap a spinal collar around her neck and splint those broken arms.

We pull away from the scene to head for hospital and as we move off I glance once more at the disarray and shake my head. Every working day I drive along this motorway and experience the anarchy of its commuters' shambolic sense of road rules, waiting for a poorly timed decision to bring traffic to a standstill. But I'd never expect to see a meth-head in a van hurtling towards me at 150km/h from the opposite direction.

It's past midnight now and we're almost halfway through the shift. The sun has gone down, and the weird stuff is ready to come out of the quiet suburban houses of the south-west while most of Sydney sleeps blissfully unaware. We're speeding towards an eye injury caused by chemical exposure in Cabramatta. It's rare, but occasionally you get a run of big, exciting jobs on the IC car. Usually, it's so busy that we become just another general duties ambulance, scooping up all the back pains and twisted ankles that are overloading the emergency services switchboard, because if one of them actually turns out to be serious, it's a bad look when there's an ambulance crew sitting around drinking coffee, even though they're meant to be reserved for high-level emergencies.

Mark and I scoot down a side path and into a unit on a battle-axe block and see two men fighting over the use of a kitchen sink in the open-plan living area. They're pushing each other out of the way, desperately trying to splash water onto their faces.

'What the hell's going on here?' I announce.

One of the men says they had been cleaning their oven and some of the caustic fumes from the cleaning agent somehow wafted into their eyes.

'Who cleans their oven at this time of night?' asks Mark.

There's no newspaper lining the bottom of the Smeg appliance that's set between the floor-level kitchen cupboards. There's no cans of Easy-Off Bam nearby. It's not a task usually shared by two dudes, either.

The men beg for help. We tell them they'll need to go to hospital. We've got no idea what chemicals are in oven cleaner and what sort of harm they can do to eyesight. They both immediately refuse, as people often do when they're up to no good. Hospital equals police to them. They want to know if there's any other option. Not that we can offer, I tell them.

'Do we *have* to go to hospital?'

'We can't force you to go or kidnap you. This isn't North Korea,' I say. 'You're grown men, you can make your own choice, but I'd strongly suggest you come. Otherwise, if you want to take your chances continuing to rinse with water, that's on you.'

The men decide to stay, and we leave them with their faces dripping onto the tiles, hoping they'll at least figure out that there's another sink in the bathroom.

'Those blokes were up to something,' I say to Mark back in the ambulance. 'I know oven cleaner has caustic soda in it. I wonder if that's used by drug manufacturers.'

Mark performs a quick Google search on his phone. 'Huh, caustic soda, a common name for sodium hydroxide, is used in a number of synthesis methods to raise the pH of methamphetamine solutions.'

There's no time to ruminate on the meth lab we just stumbled upon, or how we may end up back there later if Dumb & Dumber cause it to explode. Because a 1A springs up on the radio.

We use our searchlights on the unlit road in Austral to locate the semi-rural acreage we're looking for and rumble down its stony driveway. The house is designed in Grecian style: symmetrical fluted columns and large slabs of concrete. Another ambulance is already reversed up against the low porch at the front of the house. We head indoors and follow the clicks of a defibrillator's metronome ringing through the corridors. Voices making treatment plans become audible next. We take one last turn and find the sounds are coming from behind a huge door with a latch and rubber seal around its edges. The door makes a sucking sound as I peel it open and find a full-blown resuscitation happening inside a gigantic walk-in cool room. Floor-to-ceiling shelves are stacked with frozen meat and skinned animal carcasses dangle from hooks in the ceiling. I push one out of the way and for some reason the *Rocky* theme starts playing in my head.

The crew we're backing up is in a steady rhythm, taking turns cycling between CPR and managing the patient's airway. The lifeless man, Dimitrios, looks to be about 50 years old and is an avid hunter who stores his trophies and future meals in this arctic chamber. His wife explains that he woke after forgetting to pull meat out for the following day – and when he didn't return to bed, she knew something was wrong. She found him collapsed and unresponsive. How long he'd been there, she couldn't be sure.

The crew has used trauma shears to cut through the thick puffer jacket that Dimitrios has thrown over his pyjamas, and a plethora of once-floating feathers have now settled in random areas on the cool room floor. They're in a dilemma of climate and endurance; not knowing this arrest would be run in a cool room, they're freezing in the shirts they're wearing because no one wears a jacket to a cardiac arrest. CPR makes you far too hot. Which is the only thing keeping them warm right now, but it's also tiring. They've been cracking ribs for 10 minutes now, but we've brought relief in the form of a machine called the LUCAS. It's a mechanical device that uses a piston to deliver steady chest compressions with a consistency no human can achieve. And it never gets tired. We attach it to Dimitrios, freeing up an extra set of hands to perform treatment. We get to work – intubating, cannulating, pushing boluses of intravenous adrenaline and bags of fluid. We even try stacking some blankets to rewarm the tepid blood. But there's no response.

Mark finds a sheet and lays it over the body as it continues to lose what warmth it has left. It's an awkward place to leave a man after his sudden, unexpected death from what's likely another late-night heart attack. But we can't go moving things until the police have done their business.

I push open the sealed door to leave the cool room, ready to break the news to the family. As I do, a vacuum of air is released, lifting the sheet from the corpse. Mark squeals like a lead actress in a slasher film. I want to double over with laughter: he thinks the man has risen like Lazarus after we've just pronounced him deceased. Thankfully my professionalism kicks in. I slam the door shut again, shushing Mark, who now realises we're dealing with an air-pressure issue and not a zombie.

'Fuck mate, I thought he'd come back from the dead there,' he says. 'Scared the shit out of me.'

'That's why I'm the Iceman and you're a Goose,' I tell him.

17

WORKING STIFF

Crystal is a recurring pest for the ambulances in our area.

Mark and I spy the homeless sex worker lurking outside the main entrance to the hospital as we head back towards station after dropping off another patient at the ED. Our station is five minutes' drive from the hospital. We're inside the plant room for no more than 60 seconds, and are about to heat up our lunches, when the phone rings. It feels like a light goes off in the control room every time we open the microwave door. The dispatcher tells us we have a chest pain at the payphone one block from the hospital. The job notes tell us it's for Crystal. Her name, which couldn't be more apt for a budget-friendly, alley-trolling, Western Sydney working girl, radiates off the screen in capital letters. From the notes, we can also see she's decided to tell the call-taker that she's wearing a pink shirt and black tracksuit pants – exactly what she was wearing when we passed her outside the hospital five minutes ago.

Today will be a quick trip for her, then. Usually, Crystal is found slightly further away from her ultimate destination of the ED, at local service stations and convenience stores. Once, while putting diesel in the truck, we watched her exit the back of a silver sedan and proceed to be paid in coins by a shifty-looking bloke. She then flagged us down to ask for a bottle of water instead of going inside the servo and buying one with her vocational proceeds. It was the kind of financial savvy that would make *The Barefoot Investor* proud.

We drive back to where we've just been, and Crystal emerges from a seedy alleyway behind a kebab shop and sticks out her arm as if hailing a taxi. I roll down my window as Mark pulls up the van beside her. I ask what's wrong today and she says it's heart palpitations. I tell her it sounds serious, so we'll have to take her to hospital. I haven't even got time to get out before Crystal is opening the side door herself and clambering in the back like she does this every day. Which she does.

'Seatbelt on,' Mark calls out. 'What's been happening today, Crystal?'

'Drinkin' red wine,' she rasps with a voice of a 40-year smoker.

'Oh yeah. What sort? Merlot? Shiraz? A nice cab sav?'

Crystal croaks a laugh through her seven remaining teeth.

'Just goon,' she replies. 'How's your day been?'

'Busy as, would you believe? Seems like all this bloody dispatcher does is send us to job after job. It's like he hates us.'

'Sounds like you've pissed off your pimp.'

I spit out the gulp of water I've just taken.

'What?' I chuckle. 'Our pimp? What the hell are you talking about, Crystal?'

'This dispatcher; he tells you what to do, right?'

'Yep.'

'And he gets all the praise and recognition at the end of the day?'

'I guess.'

'But it's you guys at the frontline taking all the risks, yeah?'

'Yeah . . .'

'Then that's your pimp, baby. He owns your arse. And he will mess you up if you do wrong by him.'

'Holy shit, that's deep, Crystal,' says Mark. 'I think you missed your calling as a philosopher.'

'Actually studied philosophy at uni, would you believe?'

'No way. How'd you end up where you are now?'

'Ah, story for another day, boys. Thanks for the lift.'

And just like that she's out the side door of the ambulance and heading in through the front doors of the ED. Crystal isn't bothered about going through the normal triage process with us. She's probably just after some sandwiches and knows the first nurse she sees will grab some to keep her happy. And quiet. Crystal isn't above making a scene to get what she wants. It's easier to oblige so that the mothers in the waiting room don't have to explain to their children why the half-naked lady who's missing all the teeth is writhing on the floor, having a tantrum that would put any toddler to shame.

We're outside chatting with some other ambos who have just offloaded their patients as well when the dispatcher hails us again.

'Having some trouble finding Crystal there, guys?' he asks.

'We just drove her to the hospital and watched her go inside,' I respond. 'Like five minutes ago.'

'Well, she's just called back from the same payphone and says she's still waiting for you. We need to send a car again.'

'What is she playing at?' I say to Mark. 'We just gave her what she wanted. Why would she walk back to the payphone and call us again, just to drive her back here once more?'

'No idea how her mind works, mate. Want to go, though? We still haven't had lunch. We could grab something from that kebab shop. I'm sure Crystal won't mind waiting. She might even shout us if she's had a productive day.'

'Ha, no thanks. Think I'll take my chances with the microwave back at the station.'

The association of Crystal with that particular kebab shop has put me off it for good. Like getting ice-cream from the Coogee Bay Hotel, some things are ruined forever. The other crew we've been chatting with offer to be Crystal's next chauffeurs and tell the dispatcher they'll fetch her instead – that way, we can be kept in reserve for something more appropriate for an intensive care ambulance.

While I'm happy that lunch appears to be back on the menu, as we drive back to station, I can't help but think about all the times I've heard members of the public declare how their taxes pay our salaries. If only they could see what their taxes are paying for right now.

A full stomach from a late lunch on a 12-hour shift prepares you for an afternoon nap a lot more than it does for the next emergency. But there's no time for siestas when Tariq has abdominal pain. Because Tariq has abdominal pain every day. And, like Crystal, he calls an ambulance. Every day. He's been doing it for longer than I've been a paramedic. He must be a national record holder for the most amount of emergency department presentations. He's had every doctor, every specialist and every surgeon examine every millimetre of his gastro-intestinal tract and other abdominal organs with every scan, scope and test that modern medicine affords. And none of them have been able to identify a cause or source of his pain. Most ambos reckon he's just an opioid seeker. But if he's faking, he's a better performer than Daniel Day-Lewis. He assures us he researches the latest remedies and studies being conducted overseas and is trying to raise money to partake in them, travelling if he must. Tariq doesn't work because of his condition, so his concession card means it doesn't cost him anything for us to attend – even though any of his car-owning family members could drive him to the hospital. But if he calls, we must haul.

Tariq's front door is open, and we hear him moaning from the street as soon as the passenger door of the ambulance opens. I always wonder if this starts as soon as he hears us arrive or if it's been going for a while. Mark and Tariq haven't been getting on lately after Mark refused to give him morphine one day, so I head into the house alone. The driving paramedic is always the bad cop, too. A good driver says nothing and leaves all the talking and decision making to the treating paramedic. The downside of saying nothing is that frustration with malingerers and timewasters can cause a driver's patience to wear thin very quickly, especially a tired or hungry one. The treating paramedic always plays good cop, because ultimately, they are the one who will be stuck in the back of the ambulance with the patient. One frequent flyer is all Mark can handle today, lest he have a full-blown meltdown, so he waits in the car.

'The pain, it's back, it's back,' says Tariq as soon as I enter his room.

'I know, mate. Don't worry, I'll sort it out for you. Just got to check your blood pressure first. You know the drill.'

He holds out his arm awaiting the blood pressure cuff. I begin pumping up the cuff and Tariq starts fidgeting with a small paper bag that's sitting on the bed next to him.

'Stay still, Tariq. I've got to check your blood pressure's okay before I give you any morphine. You know that, mate.'

'Sorry. Yeah, I know. It's just I've got this now and I want to know what you think about it. Maybe we can avoid the morphine today.'

Tariq's been on and off what are known as 'management plans' for years for his use of pain relief. When his ambulance attendance becomes excessive and he's consuming opioids like an unemployed housewife consuming *Ellen*, he gets an order that says he's not to be given anything by the ambulance besides transport to hospital so that a doctor can decide what's best for him. It's being cruel to be kind because long-term opioid use is obviously terrible for the body.

From the paper bag, Tariq pulls a black box that looks like it's cologne. There's a gold stencil of a horse on it. Underneath the horse are the words *Big Stud*.

'What's this, Tariq? Calvin Klein's new fragrance?'

'No, it's a medication they've been giving me at the hospital. They rub it on my stomach. It works great. So I asked the doctor what it was. Then I went to the chemist to see if I could buy it myself. This is what he gave me.'

I flip the box and see the drug name written on the back: lignocaine.

Lignocaine is what's called a sodium channel blocker. Basically, this means it works at the cellular level in the body to stop neurons firing super-fast when bad stuff is happening, like pain. Hence it's use as a local anaesthetic.

You'll find it in some throat lozenges or topical creams for muscle aches. We use it as paramedics to treat patients in extremely dangerous cardiac rhythms to settle their heart when it gets over-excited and tries to kill them. Drug dealers are quite partial to it as well – its numbing effects and affordability mean cocaine can be cut with it to produce the same sensation without the consumer knowing they're being ripped off.

But *Big Stud* is something else entirely. And it finally clicks what. Lignocaine also has another use; its local numbing properties can treat premature ejaculation.

'Tariq, this is for your dick. You know that, right?'

A sheepish look comes across his face.

'The chemist said that's the only lignocaine he had,' Tariq replies. 'He said if I use too much it might give me a heart attack, too. That's why I wanted to ask you about it.'

'Tariq, Tariq, Tariq.' I'm shaking my head in amused disapproval. 'This will definitely kill you if you use too much of it.'

'Well how much should I use? You're the expert.'

'Trust me, mate, I'm by no means the world's greatest lover, but this is not my area of expertise.'

'What's taking so long?' calls Mark from the front yard.

'Oh, you're working with *him*,' says Tariq.

'Don't worry, Tariq,' I say. 'He's just the driver today. Come out to the car and we'll get you that morphine.'

'Oh. Yeah.'

Tariq's pain had apparently disappeared during our conversation about *Big Stud*. But now, suddenly, it's back.

'Then we'll ask the doctor at hospital if it's safe for you to rub this stuff on your tummy and how much of it you need.'

'Okay. Deal,' he replies.

Mark's waiting for us in Tariq's garden. My partner raises his arms in the air as if to say *what took so long*. I hand him the box of *Big Stud*.

'What the hell is this? *Ohhh*.'

Inside the ambulance, Tariq gets his morphine. He isn't currently on a management plan, so if he asks for pain relief, he gets it – as long as his treating paramedic is in a good mood. Luckily, Mark is the driver today. Tariq's veins are so frequently used by other paramedics, it's like there's pre-drilled pilot holes in the crook of his elbow. I don't even bother applying a tourniquet, he's so easy to cannulate. Not long after, the warm embrace of opium poppy extract floods Tariq's central nervous system and we enjoy a quiet ride to the hospital.

So quiet, in fact, I need to force myself from drifting off into an afternoon nap.

18

CULTURE SHOCKING

The shrill ringtone of the station phone pierces through the air of the reclining area, entering my head like a captive bolt to the brain. The ability of this sound to inflict searing pain into your temples is unparalleled; when the night is becoming morning's early hours, you're exhausted from what the shift has pummelled you with, and you've just laid down to rest and entered some strange phase of REM sleep where you're neither asleep nor awake.

My first reaction in this situation is always a loud groan, followed by a glance at the time. As my eyes adjust to the dark to read my watch, another moan escapes from somewhere deep in my throat. It's 4.15am. Only 15 minutes have passed since we rolled into the station for the first time tonight. We've only just unzipped our boots and sprawled out on the couches to grab whatever sleep we can. Collapsing from exhaustion and slipping into the initial phases of unconsciousness, only to be woken moments later by the shriek of an ambulance station phone, is far worse than not catching z's at all. It's a cruel form of sleep-deprivation torture, ripped right out of the playbook of an SAS selection course.

Stumbling over to answer the call, if for no other reason than to silence the unholy noise, my brain still isn't alert enough to send signals to my mouth to form complete words.

'Liv'pool station,' I grumble.

The dispatcher, who's no doubt fluent in Drowsy Paramedic, doesn't say much because he doesn't need to.

'Hey mate, 1A for you guys.'

'Copy, no worries,' I reply, hanging up the receiver before I've barely finished the sentence.

No time for small talk.

As I've mentioned before, 1A is our highest priority case – cardiac arrest. The caller has told the 000 operator that the patient has stopped breathing. In our geographical area, this isn't necessarily always the case – people have a lot of interpretations of what breathing is. Sometimes the caller and the patient are one in the same – yes, some people will call in their own cardiac arrest – and they tell the 000 operator that they themselves are, in fact, dead. Febrile convulsions in children are another common one, where an infant has a seizure when a fever from an uncontrolled infection spikes too high. First-time parents seeing their new child's whole body stiffen and turn blue usually earn a 1A from their panicked voices on the phones. Notes that come through the MDT mentioning a fever are usually enough to make us feel relieved, though. We know febrile convulsions usually self-resolve in less than a minute and can be dealt with by keeping up regular children's Panadol.

The alert to my partner is even more concise than the dispatcher.

'Dave . . . 1A,' I say.

I say it just loud enough to wake the human-sized lump that's hiding under a blanket and facing the other direction on a recliner. A lump that's already gone back into a deep slumber. Dave's got 15 years on me, has three kids and spent 15 years in the army before becoming a civilian ambo, so he knows how precious sleep is and the techniques used to grab it. Sleep when you can because you don't know if you'll get another chance. That was the army expression. Dave was a combat medic in Afghanistan, so the south-west is like a holiday for him. He's an incredible teacher and has high expectations. But he's also ice-cold calm in a crisis and blessed with a scathing sense of sarcasm.

I'm out into the plant room and ticking over the engine before Dave's boots are back on. As I punch the address into the GPS, he staggers through the passenger-side door.

'How old?' he asks.

Always the first thing every paramedic wants to know on a cardiac arrest.

'Two.'

'Shit.'

'What?'

'Nothing, I just hate it when it's a kid.'

'Yeah, probably just a febrile seizure, though.'

The address is over in Fairfield, so it's a decent run, but owing to the minimal traffic at this time of night, we should be there in less than 10 minutes.

'Nothing in the notes about a fever,' Dave mutters as I steadily increase our driving speed on the first main road out of the station.

Dave jots down notes and numbers that we'll need to treat the patient, based on their age and ideal weight: IV adrenaline doses, endotracheal tube size, electricity in joules for defibrillation.

I shift my gaze back to the road and have a brief panic attack; I'm closing in on a speed camera I've driven past at least a thousand times before. Never at this pace, though. It's acceptable for us to break the speed limit by 30km/h or so. But I'm doing 140km/h. In a 60km/h zone. Now it's me yelling *shit* as the night's dark haze is bleached white by the camera's phosphorescent flash.

'I'm sure the boss will let you out of this one,' says Dave. 'As long as you're not smiling in the picture.'

I've never driven this fast in relation to the speed limit to a job before, and I'm not intending to either. But a subconscious sense of urgency has made the speedo's needle creep up faster than it normally would, and the lack of geriatrics in Toyota Camrys and pedestrians at crossings on the night-time asphalt obscures my sense of speed. The ride feels smooth, like the van is gliding on rails to our destination.

The data terminal squawks again with new notes. Police have arrived at the scene and radioed through that the child is conscious and breathing. My right foot instantly eases off the accelerator. The dispatcher asks if we've seen the new information. Dave picks up the radio and replies that we have and that it's good news. He lets her know we're only a couple of minutes away.

I keep the beacons on until we turn into the street we're looking for – no need to blind everyone with LEDs – and we pull in behind another ambulance. Our colleagues have gotten here first. They must have been on their way back to station from a previous job. They haven't reported anything on the radio yet, though. They've either just arrived, or the patient isn't that unwell and they're taking their time.

It's the former. And the police were wrong. Very wrong.

An infant boy lies motionless in the centre of the living room, ringed by two scrambling paramedics, a hysterical mother and some confused-looking police officers. The boy's eyes are open, his mouth agape, lips popping apart at irregular intervals in the same motion a goldfish makes to take breaths when it surfaces. But these aren't real, effective breaths. They're called agonal respirations – a gasping brainstem reflex that symbolises the body making a last-ditch effort for oxygen, and a tell-tale sign of cardiac arrest.

The cops' mistake is understandable. This is a sight few people are ever confronted with and even some with medical training would confuse this for real breathing. But as soon as Dave and I see the kid, we know he has no heartbeat. His pale, mottled complexion indicates skin that has no blood being pumped to it because his heart has stopped working.

It's little wonder the crew we're backing up – Richard and Steph – hadn't radioed anything through in the moments they had with the patient before we arrived. Precious seconds talking on a radio are better utilised treating a patient with no heartbeat. Steph is ripping apart the compartments of the LifePak 15 monitor to find the defibrillator pads. She places them on the boy's chest and back. Richard is hooking up the bag mask from their OxyViva so he can start breathing for the patient. As the second defibrillator pad sticks onto the boy's skin, and Steph flicks the monitor into 'Paddles' mode to assess what rhythm his heart is in, none of us can believe the frenzy of acid-green squiggles firing across the monitor's LCD screen. It's VF – ventricular fibrillation – one of two rhythms that can be shocked by a defibrillator, and therefore have the potential for a positive outcome. It's an unmistakable rhythm because of the disjointed flurry of electrical activity that sets it apart from every other heart rhythm, which have some degree of order to them. We're in disbelief because children who go into cardiac arrest are never in a shockable rhythm; they're always in asystole – the infamous flatline. And they almost never survive. VF arrests are for 50-year-olds who collapse when they're out for a jog because a piece of pork has blocked one of their coronary arteries.

'Okay, let's start doing CPR and charge up the monitor,' I say from the doorway. 'And make sure it's set to 50 joules.'

Kids' bodies can't handle as much electricity as adults can, hence why we need to be mindful to decrease the joules from its default setting of 200 joules, and hence Dave's fastidious notes on the way here.

'Charging!' Steph calls out, as the familiar wind-up siren tone of a LifePak rings through the house.

It's the only sound being made right now besides the gentle exertion of a police officer doing CPR. Everyone else is quiet. Watching. And waiting.

'Okay, hands off,' Steph tells the cop doing compressions. 'And . . . shocking!'

The jolt of electricity gives the boy's lifeless body a violent contraction before it returns to its comatose state. Dave instructs the police officer to continue with chest compressions.

'Should we just get him in the car and start heading for hospital?' a voice behind me questions.

It's Edward, the duty supervisor for the night. He's obviously seen the job go down on his management software and decided to attend for the welfare of the crews and family. Additionally, even though he's an intensive care paramedic himself, he can help by adopting a scene management and logistics role. The clinical part of the job gets left to us.

'Good idea,' I reply.

I pass the thought onto Dave, and he concurs as well.

There's a morbid reason why we rapidly extricate and transport little ones who are in cardiac arrest. It's because we know they're going to die despite everything we do. Kids who go into cardiac arrest rarely – if ever – come out of it. And parents shouldn't be left to recall the image of their lifeless child every time they look at their bed or the living room floor or wherever it was they collapsed. No, if a child must die, it should be in a hospital. Because hospitals are where people die. And specialist paediatric hospitals offer far superior support services to grieving parents than anything a few bumbling paramedics and police could ever hope to achieve.

Dave scoops the boy into his left arm and does CPR with his right as he dashes for our ambulance. Steph trails behind carrying the LifePak, the cables of which are still attached to the boy. We pile into the intensive care ambulance because it's already set up with the extra gear we'll need for this patient.

Dave's the treating officer tonight, so he fires off instructions. He gets Steph to take over CPR and Richard to prepare for the next rhythm check, while he sets up to intubate. My job is to find IV access, a notoriously tricky task on infants at the best of times due to their chubbier limbs. The task is further complicated because cardiac arrest means minimal blood flow to engorge veins and make them visible.

But I have a different idea, in the form of a shiny new toy we've just been given in the previous weeks. It's the same bone-drill I saw the doctor use way back when I was a trainee, crapping my pants with the patient who tried to saw off his neck with a kitchen knife. The EZ-IO drill, as it's known, has been around for years, but our ambulance service has only recently acquired them.

Hands quivering, I draw the gun from its pouch in our treatment kit and fit the paediatric drill-bit to it. I've used the drill twice so far, but that's been on adults. I've never bored into a two-year-old's fragile tibia bone with this barbaric instrument.

The needle tip pierces the fatty flesh just below the infant's left knee and abruptly stops when it collides with bone cortex. This is my signal that I've hit the right landmark and it's time to squeeze the trigger. The drill whirs no differently than a Ryobi from Bunnings and, with a few pounds of extra pressure from a gentle push, does the same job. I feel a loss of resistance as the needle drops another centimetre and comes to rest in the marrow of the child's tibia.

'Got access,' I announce to the crew.

'Holy shit, was that a drill?' says a cop watching on through the back doors of the ambulance.

With this access port, we can now start giving adrenaline to get the kid's heart going again, no differently than we would through normal intravenous access.

'Time for the next rhythm check,' Dave calls from the head of the stretcher. 'Charging . . . hands off . . . Okay, VF again. Shocking!'

Another surge of lightning snaps through the patient, and I switch places with Steph to take over CPR while she starts to draw up the adrenaline. My right palm bounces up and down on the kid's breastbone while my left hand braces on my right wrist so I don't compress too hard. Paediatric CPR needs to be far more delicate than with adults.

Then something strange happens. The kid starts crying.

'What the fuuu . . .' I mutter quietly, conscious of the fact I'm near a child, albeit one who's clinically dead.

I stop my compressions. It seems like the kid is alive again. But then as soon as I stop, he becomes lifeless. I glance at the monitor. It's still showing VF – a rhythm it's impossible to be alive in. You can't be conscious, have a pulse, or be crying in VF. If you are in VF, you are dead. No argument.

'What are you doing?' snaps Dave.

'Sorry, I thought we had him back,' I say, feeling stupid as the words leave my mouth.

I begin compressions again. Dave continues to fiddle with his intubation gear and is ready to insert the breathing tube. But I tell him to stop. I want him to see what I'm seeing before I make another crazy statement.

'Look mate, he's bloody crying!'

Everyone collectively gasps, and I stop my compressions yet again because I feel like I'm torturing this kid while simultaneously trying to save his life. The monitor continues to frazzle with the erratic spikes of VF.

'You just need to keep doing compressions,' Dave says.

I agree and continue, somewhat uncomfortably. There's no treatment for VF besides chest compressions and defibrillation, and with our rhythm checks being every two minutes, it's at least another minute until we can shock again.

Groans dribble from the child's mouth and his eyes stream, but I can't stop CPR – it would only be detrimental. I'm in the throes of another extremely rare phenomenon: CPR-induced consciousness. Being both alive and dead at the same time.

For years, other paramedics have told tales of patients trying to push them off while having CPR. They'd claim it felt like it was the patient's ghostly way of saying they didn't want to be revived. I always thought these episodes were complete horse shit and added into yarns as pure embellishment – as is so often the case in the traded war stories of paramedics. Now I'm one of the converted.

Dave announces the next rhythm check, bringing my mind back into focus. He charges the defibrillator and when the tone reaches its crescendo, the obligatory *hands off* command rings through the vehicle to make sure no one gets shocked who doesn't need to be. I lift my hands in anticipation of dropping them straight back onto the kid's chest to continue compressing.

'Non-shockable, dumping the charge,' says Dave, interrupting the process.

Non-shockable means one of two things: either the patient has gone into asystole, signifying matters have worsened, or the spikes on the LifePak's LED screen have arranged themselves into some sort of order. Which suggests there might be a heartbeat.

'Potentially perfusing, check for a pulse,' orders Dave, placing two fingers where the child's carotid artery should be.

I check the femoral artery. And it's bounding.

'Got a pulse,' I say.

'Me too,' says Dave.

The cops cheer with excitement. The child's mother is praising her god. No such celebrations come from any of us paramedics though. We're not out of the woods yet. We know someone can fall back into cardiac arrest just as quickly as they've come out of it without proper post-ROSC* care. The body's oxygenation is likely to be poor, so intubation may still be required. IV fluids may be needed to restore blood pressure. And something has caused the cardiac arrest. We need to figure out what that is. And in this case, we have no clue. The child's mother's English is poor, and her story is vague.

We make the decision to bolt for the children's hospital. Richard drives, Dave and I stay in the back with the patient, and Steph takes his mother in the other ambulance. The

---

* Return of spontaneous circulation: when the body can sustain a perfusing heart rhythm on its own after a cardiac arrest. This can't be achieved without intervention, usually CPR and defibrillation.

police escort us with a 'green light corridor', ensuring an uninterrupted, speedy journey.

We continue treatment on the way. I get some IV fluids running and Dave assists the child's breathing with the bag-valve mask. His level of consciousness has come up remarkably high and he doesn't require intubation. He's even starting to open his eyes and make sounds. We let the hospital know via the radio what we're bringing and are certain every other ambulance out there is listening in to hear what we've been up to.

When we arrive at the hospital, we're greeted by a legion of doctors and nurses; I've never seen this many waiting for one patient. The head specialist has an instant look of recognition on his face. He's treated the patient for a cardiac arrest before.

'You mean this kid has had *two* cardiac arrests?' I ask.

'Yep, he's definitely getting his own internal defibrillator this time,' he replies.

'How does this happen? To a two-year-old?'

'Consanguineous parents, mate. Mum and dad are blood related. He's got a rare congenital heart defect that can cause all sorts of issues.'

'You wouldn't get that anywhere else but in the south-west,' says Dave when we're debriefing back at our ambulances outside.

And sadly, he's got a point. Us paramedics know from experience in treating paediatric patients with obscure conditions that consanguineous relationships are far more common than they should be in south-west Sydney. But it was his congenital heart defect that put him into a shockable rhythm instead of the normally un-shockable asystole: in some strange way, the same thing that killed our patient tonight also saved his life. Again.

19

CHILD SUPPORT

'You're taking my kid to the private hospital, or you're not getting out of this house.'

Using his hulking frame, the father blocks any escape we have through the front door. He's pissed off. And none of us have any idea why.

The Ambulance Gods are angry with us too, it seems; they've dispatched us to another child who supposedly isn't breathing immediately after the harrowing ordeal we've just been through. But as soon as Steph, Richard, Dave and I bowl into the house, we can all see there's no cause for alarm this time. Or, more accurately, we can *hear* that everything is alright.

A small girl, about four years old, sits staring at us from the living room lounge. Her colour is good, her breathing rate normal and she looks totally relaxed. But every so often a loud cough, said countless times in medical textbooks and lectures to resemble that of a barking seal, emerges from her tiny body. It's a sound that terrifies naïve new parents, but gives nothing more than a sense of welcome relief to seasoned paramedics who've been told they're responding to a paediatric who isn't breathing.

The girl has croup – an extremely common viral infection of the upper airway that mostly affects children between the ages of about two and six. And new parents always call ambulances for it. And it's always in the early hours of the morning. And they always say the child can't breathe or isn't breathing. Luckily, croup is rarely serious. It isn't really a breathing problem; it's mostly just a cough. A nasty-sounding cough nevertheless and, sometimes, a grating wheezy sound as well that's called stridor, which is the result of inflammation in an undeveloped airway. Croup rarely requires hospitalisation; a simple course of steroids fixes it in a matter of days. Unfortunately, we don't carry those steroids, so we usually offer a trip to hospital anyway, after which the child is promptly discharged once a doctor has seen them. Most parents gratefully accept our offer and happily pop their child on their lap for the ride to the big sick bay. But not this father.

He's angered by the fact we can't take his child to a private hospital of his choice, an option he feels entitled to from paying for private health insurance. No matter how much we try to explain that we are a public service that transports only to public hospitals, coupled with the fact that private hospitals don't have all-hours emergency departments and are really only for non-urgent surgeries and rehab, he isn't buying it. So much so that he's now threatening us.

It's another stark reminder of the difference between providing healthcare in an uncontrolled environment, as opposed to inside the safe walls of a hospital. For us paramedics, there's no spare hands to run upstairs and retrieve from the storeroom if you haven't done your due diligence when checking your gear at the start of shift and a piece of equipment is missing or a medication is out of date. You're stuffed. And there's no security guards to protect you if a patient or a family member's mood takes a turn for the worse. You're left to fight your own battle, which sometimes turns physical.

'Mate, the only way she's going to a private hospital is if you drive her yourself. And even then, once you get there, I guarantee you they'll tell you to go to the public ED anyway,' I tell the enraged man.

'AND WHAT IF SOMETHING HAPPENS TO HER WHILE I'M DRIVING THERE?' he roars back at me.

He's still not moving away from the door frame. Even though there's four of us, I don't like our odds of taking him on or making it past him. He's what Big Phil would look like if he had a normal diet that was supplemented by bikie-enforcer levels of injectable testosterone. He looks like Jack Reacher ate Dwayne Johnson.

Out of the corner of my eye, I spy Dave fidgeting. I remember he's ex-army and imagine there's the sounds of helicopters and gunfire being triggered in the part of his brain where the war in Afghanistan has been locked away. He's giving away a lot of size, but Dave isn't scared of this bloke. He's bellicose, but he also doesn't have his M4 assault rifle on him right now. Then he surprises me.

'You're right, mate,' Dave says. 'What if something *does* happen on the way? There's a public hospital a few minutes' drive from here, but the private hospital is at least 15. You hear that sound she's making? That's her airway closing. I'm the most senior paramedic here and if that airway fully closes and she stops breathing, there's nothing I can do for her. She'll need a doctor to perform a surgical airway, and they've got plenty of those at the hospital down the road. But if you make us drive somewhere that's three times further, and she goes downhill when we could've already been at a hospital, that'll be on you. And you'll never be able to live with yourself. I've got a daughter that's around her age as well, and I know I wouldn't.'

The man opens his mouth to reply, as if he's about to finally agree and let us get on with our job, having succumbed to Dave's mildly white lie. But before any words can come out, his entire body slams face-first onto the floor tiles directly in front of him.

A police officer has kicked in the door, which promptly slammed into the father's back and knocked him flat.

The cop piles into the house with two of his colleagues. All have their guns drawn and pointed at the father on the floor. The little girl squeals. The cops kneel on the man, pin him down and handcuff him. Dave, Richard and I look around in disbelief. Steph just holds up her portable radio and points to the little red distress button that discreetly activates help for us when we're in danger.

'Good thing one of us has some situational awareness,' she says.

The young girl is chaperoned by her mother for the drive to hospital. And the junior police constable sits in the back with me. It's a quiet ride, the silence only occasionally broken by an intermittent croak from the patient, who's still suffering from croup. They say that the more comfortable you are with someone, the less need there is to fill the silence. But I've got nothing more to say to this woman given the way her husband thought it was acceptable to treat paramedics. And her lack of communication certainly isn't coming from a feeling of comfort right now.

We pull into the ambulance bay and Dave wheels the stretcher holding the patient and her mother inside the hospital. I wander over to the triage nurse. I don't even need to give a full handover. She's already heard the barking cough.

'Croup?' she asks.

'Yep,' I reply.

'Vaccinations up to date?'

'Oh yeah, I forgot to ask about that in all the kerfuffle, which I'll tell you about later. Is she vaccinated?' I call over to the mother.

'No, we're not going to vaccinate our kids.'

'Of course not,' the nurse mumbles under her breath. 'Fucking idiots. We've given up even trying with these people anymore. They probably won't even give the kid the Redipred* the doctor tells them to use.'

'May as well get the doc to write a prescription for salt crystals and mud,' I say.

'Yep, this one is the Darwin award winner for today. Seriously, these anti-vaxxers are going to undo the hundreds of years of work medical science has done for us.'

'Ha, the world would really need to go to shit for that to happen; I can't imagine it.'

'Yeah, seems unlikely. Anyway, sun's coming up. This will be your last patient for the shift, won't it? Are you back on tonight?'

'No, this is it. Start of my days off,' I say.

'Got any plans for tomorrow, then?'

'Why, should I? What's tomorrow?'

'Australia Day.'

'Oh yeah, it's the 25th today.'

Dates and days of the week get muddled in a blur of time when you're a paramedic. It's either a work day or it isn't. In a way, our life calendars are simplified by the odd nature of shift work. But it also means we're less likely to know the day of the week than a dementia patient with low blood sugar.

---

* Brand name for the common preparation of prednisolone used to treat croup in children.

But today is a day we'll never forget. A day that will change history.

The 25th. Of January. 2020.

A date that means nothing to me right now but will soon be remembered as the day that would change healthcare in Australia forever.

20

GOING VIRAL

On 25 January 2020, a bloke arrives in Melbourne, stepping off a plane from a place called Wuhan.

This time last week, no one I know had even heard of the place. But now a microscopic smuggler from this faraway city has snuck aboard with this man and is about to break the nation's healthcare system and change Australia for good.

We've heard vague reports about a new flu spreading in China: a few people are dying from a strange new variant of pneumonia. A city might have been locked down. The odd nurse or doctor brings it up in conversation. A few news reports mention it. But every paramedic dismisses coronavirus as though it's nothing to be concerned about, and everyone in healthcare is already an expert on the subject.

'It's just like SARS and swine-flu, hardly anyone died from those, and they just went away eventually. They never came here.'

'You've got to be stuck in a room with someone for five hours to catch it.'

'Young people don't die from viruses. It'll just get caught by a few in the nursing homes like influenza does every year and that'll be it.'

We make jokes with patients who call us for respiratory issues. We're used to multiple calls for shortness of breath every day. People coughing up phlegm from minor bacterial chest infections and bouts of anxiety are the most common ones. Very occasionally we might get a legitimate respiratory emergency, like a severe asthma attack or pulmonary oedema – but these are in the handfuls each year. But now we find ourselves adding in a question about recent travel to China. It's not a requirement. It's just a hilarious gag to us at this stage.

'Haven't been to China recently by any chance?' we say to Mavis, a 93-year-old bed-bound grandmother who hasn't left the house in 20 years.

Patients and family members cackle along with us.

We even jest about the dispatchers sending our more experienced colleagues to respiratory cases.

'Don't send Terry, he's old! He might not come back from this one!'

No one is even contemplating wearing masks right now. We don't even know where we keep them in the ambulance. Or if we do at all. Masks have only ever been used by surgeons or Slipknot members. Eye protection might get put on when a stabbing or shooting victim is spraying claret like a firehose. Which is not very often. Half the time I don't even wear gloves if the patient looks clean enough.

This pantomime goes on for a month.

Then COVID claims its first victim in Australia, after a literal boatload of people on a luxury cruise ship called the *Diamond Princess,* which contains a bunch of Aussies, becomes a hotbed of disease. Then it claims another victim. And another.

Still, we're not bothered. It's business as usual. It's just a few people. Thousands die of influenzas in Australia every year. And that doesn't make the news or raise any eyebrows.

Then the World Health Organization tells us that coronavirus is a worldwide pandemic.

We're more distracted with arguing over whether the Chinese government deliberately brewed this thing up in a lab before unleashing it on the world, or if someone bought a live bat at a place called a wet market and took it home to have sex with it.

Then they cancel the Formula One. And the rugby league.

Do what you want, but don't take our bloody sport away from us.

On the upside, Tom Hanks infects Richard Wilkins.

Within days, the country is swept by a barrage of previously unheard-of phrases that are flung out by the media, like *social distancing* and *self-isolation,* and things start getting really weird. All sport is off. Completely. Doesn't matter if it's weekend netball or top-level Aussie rules. Pubs are shut. Gyms are closed. Restaurants, cafes and cinemas are gone, too. We can't gather in crowds. Australians can't travel anywhere. No one can travel to Australia. We're supposed to wear masks and keep our distance from other people as if they've got leprosy. There's talk of closing schools.

Who's going to run the hospitals and go to emergencies if all the doctors and nurses and ambos are at home looking after their kids because schools are shut? we think.

State premiers are holding daily press conferences and the nation watches on as the number of COVID cases bounces up and down.

Then the monolithic incubator known as the *Ruby Princess* dumps its COVID-riddled contents onto our shores. Then no one can leave the house. Except to go to work if we're considered essential workers or to go shopping. Maniacs abuse the rules and buy nothing except bulk packs of toilet paper and dry pasta. The viral apocalypse is getting serious.

The daily news conferences don't have any blips on the south-west Sydney regions of their maps yet, though. We're still safe, we think.

Then the strangest thing of all happens. Something amazing.

The phone stops ringing.

For two weeks, crews in the south-west start seeing time on station with only the occasional call-out for a legitimate emergency. My partner Angus and I, on the intensive care car, make it through an entire series of a new Netflix show called *Tiger King* in a single day, and come away thinking how grateful we are to be paramedics in south-west Sydney – and not the lawless Deep South of America. This coronavirus is the best thing that's ever happened to us, we think quietly to ourselves. Everyone has finally recognised ambulances for the four-wheeled Petri dishes they are and are bothering us only when they really need to, because if anyone is carrying coronavirus around, it's most likely us. We're the only ones who can leave the house, except when people need to get a COVID test or join the JobSeeker queue – where everyone is stacked on top of each other and not wearing masks. We see this and, as apprehensive as we are about the direction our job is heading, we're thankful we still have a job.

We see colleagues in the Eastern Suburbs boarding police boats, dressed in full hazmat sperm suits, ferrying people off cruise liners and into what are being called 'quarantine hotels'. We can't believe it; normally it's us in the south-west getting screwed over with the worst jobs.

Then the dream dies.

Angus and I attend our first patient with coronavirus. It's an elderly gentleman who's fallen out of bed. That's what our dispatch notes say anyway. What his daughter hasn't told the 000-operator is that the reason he fell out of bed is because he's severely short of breath. We haven't seen or heard anyone with coronavirus before, but from the limited information we've read on the internet, we know it can cause pulmonary oedema – or excessive fluid – in the lungs, a condition immediately identifiable by breathing that sounds like the person is being forced to talk while being waterboarded with a bowl of Rice Bubbles.

We take one look at him and retreat to the ambulance. With the information we've been given, all we've brought in with us are gloves, a first aid kit and some observation equipment. We clearly need the protection we've seen the ambos on TV wearing. The man could be seconds from cardiac arrest, but we need to protect ourselves. We apologise to the man's daughter but tell her there's nothing we can do until we're fully gowned-up, with face-masks and goggles as well. She assures us he doesn't have coronavirus, despite him displaying the most obvious of symptoms, as so many patients and family members will continue to do for the duration of this plague without any way of knowing or proving. But we're taking no chances. We're seeing the death toll pile up on the news every day, and we want to do everything possible to keep this thing away from ourselves and our families.

It's nearing the end of the summer months, so the temperature is still balmy. We unfold the yellow plastic gowns for the first time and cloak ourselves in them, and it doesn't take long for sweat to start seeping down our foreheads and fogging up our protective goggles. Perspiration pools in the fingertips of our gloves. We wonder how this is going to be sustainable.

We trounce back into the apartment, up two flights of stairs and load the man onto our stair-chair: a collapsible, rudimentary device that's to be avoided when possible. It's an endless source of nuisance and back injuries, and is only to be brought out when the patient absolutely cannot walk. Now it's just another place for germs to infest.

The difficulties of carrying the man down the stairs are now multiplied exponentially by the plastic bin bags we're now wrapped in, and Angus can't get his off quickly enough once we load the patient into the back of the ambulance. He's a hairy, sweaty bloke at the best of times. Now he's a six-foot, bearded Border Collie that's just spent 20 minutes in a sauna.

And it's a whole new endeavour fraught with infectious hazards as well, this PPE business. Once your gloves have touched a surface or a patient, they're contaminated, and so henceforth is everything they come into contact with: door handles, radios, car keys. You can't reach under your gown to grab your stethoscope or look at your watch or grab your medication booklet. And removing the PPE must be done in the correct order, under immense heat and stress and complaining about taking too long from the patient, so that a contaminated glove or finger doesn't accidentally contact a clean patch of skin or hair. Then you must dispose of the dirty PPE somewhere. This means putting on another pair of clean gloves over your sweaty, shrivelled fingers. It's like Clive Palmer trying to squeeze into a pair of medium jeans.

We're on our way to the ED, so I radio ahead and let them know we're bringing in a patient with coronavirus. Then, mid-sentence, I notice something change on the probe that's been measuring the man's oxygen saturation, but also measures a patient's heart rate. His pulse drops from 70 to 30. That's way too low, unless you're Lance Armstrong at his doping peak. Then I remember something his daughter told us back in the unit. He skipped his kidney dialysis appointment yesterday because he couldn't be bothered going.

'Shit! It's bloody hyperkalaemia*,' I say.

'How do you know?' says Angus.

'Because the ECG I'm about to do will confirm it.'

I haven't done an ECG on the man because I've been trying to contaminate as little equipment as possible with coronavirus. Hell, I haven't even put oxygen on him because I don't want a high-flow, non-rebreather mask blowing deadly spores all around the confined cabin.

I stick electrodes all over the man's limbs and chest and, sure enough, when the monitor spits out a rhythm strip, the wide and bizarre electrical waves it prints out show that this isn't coronavirus at all. I give the man an

---

* Hyperkalaemia is a deadly condition caused by excess potassium in the blood. To give a super-nerdy physiology lesson, basically it happens when diabetes is managed poorly, a dialysis appointment gets skipped, or something really heavy crushes one of your limbs – causing billions of microscopic cells to be squished and leak all their contents (chiefly potassium) into the blood. It can be identified by certain patterns on the squiggly lines on the ECG monitor, and by physical responses too, such as shortness of breath and fluid in the lungs.

IV injection of calcium and sodium bicarbonate to start correcting the excess potassium in his system and apologise for my misdiagnosis to the team waiting for us at the hospital. They're more relieved than annoyed – the hospital system still hasn't had time, or funding, to start properly quarantining infectious patients when they arrive. Nobody knows how to implement a procedure for transferring care from an ambulance, with a patient actively being treated, with two possibly now-infected paramedics, to a team of doctors and nurses, without infecting all of them, who then could go on to infect the rest of the staff and patients in the hospital. There's no *Star Trek*-esque airlocks in these ancient buildings. Surely this will be addressed soon, we think.

Angus and I learn a valuable lesson, though: the fear is real and, if the future is cloaked in masks and gowns, it's going to suck. Big time.

The health system braces itself as confirmed cases and deaths caused by COVID-19 continue to rise every day. Intensive care units are beginning to fill up with patients on ventilators and, at the exponential rate cases are growing, seem to be destined for imminent overflow. There won't be any room left in public hospitals for the ordinary emergencies that are still going to occur every day: strokes, heart attacks, overdoses, motor-vehicle accidents. They're going to be inundated with people whose lungs have been savaged by this mysterious, mould-breaking virus and need to be kept on ventilators for weeks. Private hospitals cancel their surgeries and prepare to become makeshift EDs. Dentists and GPs fear they're going to be called in from the comfort of their country clubs to start intubating dirty serfs who don't have private health cover. I arrange a DNR – I don't want a dentist intubating me. Paramedics, one of the few groups deemed 'essential' and able to leave the house to work, are potentially being exposed to this virus all day, every day. We don't know which patients or colleagues might have it, or what surfaces it could be lingering on. If we all go down with it, we're screwed. Contingency plans are drawn up to have student paramedics – who have no ability or experience in treating patients – chauffer us around if we start dropping.

Then it comes.

The virus seeps out of the Eastern Suburbs, and it hits the patients first. Then it hits us.

It was inevitable. Donning and doffing extensive amounts of PPE and scrubbing every inch of an ambulance with disinfectant, only to go straight back out and get every inch contaminated again, is still a new concept to us. A vaccine is a distant pipedream. The residents of the south-west are ignoring household restrictions. The streets are empty, but living rooms are full of people who aren't where they should be.

People ignore health officials and laws, suggesting they are being controlled by the government and that their freedoms are being taken away. Then they get sick and call for the same public health system, whose advice they ignored, to help them in the form of an ambulance. They still call when it's not an emergency, as usual. Coughs, colds, fevers and sore throats – the basic symptoms that people are told to stay at home and recover from – become the norm. When we arrive on the scene, we tell them if you haven't got COVID, then you probably do now.

'What?' they respond.

'Who do you think is out there all day and all night exposed to the virus, carrying it around on our uniforms and equipment?' we reply.

They can't get rid of us quickly enough.

People call wanting a quick test from us, just to make sure that this cough isn't 'The 'Rona'. They're oblivious to the fact that if everyone called ambulances for tests, how the hell would we have time to get to the usual emergencies. Just when we thought the out-of-hospital world couldn't get any dumber, it proves us wrong again. You'd never see people calling the cops to make a noise complaint to arrest their baby for crying too loudly. Especially if the consequence of doing so meant spreading a deadly disease around the city.

We're absolutely obliterated by coronavirus. While ordinary citizens endure the startling new reality of lockdown, being stuck at home with their spouses and children, baking sourdough and doing push ups, they're blissfully unaware of the chaos in the healthcare world. It's non-stop patient transports, COVID and non-COVID, in full PPE, working in constant fear of being exposed. It's 15-hour shifts and then avoiding our families when we get home until our dirty uniforms are sequestered away and we're satisfactorily scrubbed clean from head to toe.

A fringe group of morons decide that now is the perfect time to start taking over capital cities in mass gatherings and protesting, inevitably increasing the spread of coronavirus and amplifying our workload exponentially. I want to tell them that if they want to make a bunch of noise and achieve nothing, then they should just join a CrossFit gym.

We drop a bunch of our routine treatments to minimise risk. No one gets nebulisers, no one gets intubated, and no one gets CPR performed anymore until we seal their airway with a mask. We hear that some American agencies stop doing CPR altogether because the danger is too high, and the outcome is unlikely to be favourable.

The precautions, while necessary, aren't foolproof. And we can't just stop treating patients altogether. So we start catching COVID. It's only a few paramedics, but contact tracing means it decimates the workforce. Rumours suggest that there are now more than 200 infected and close-contact paramedics from the south-west in isolation. It's all over the news, but it doesn't stop the trivial calls. Crews from other sectors get dragged into the Bermuda Triangle of south-west Sydney more frequently than they already are – and they're predictably unhappy about it. Call logs back up with no way of differentiating the legitimate emergencies from the time-wasters. It takes us hours to even get dispatched to some patients.

It lasts two-and-a-half months, but it feels like a year. Victoria continues to get hammered – going in and out of lockdowns. But through a combination of community compliance and sheer luck, NSW gets its COVID cases down to zero. And somehow keeps them there. Vaccine trials are sounding promising. Pubs and parks and restaurants have their restrictions gradually eased. Tap beer flows and footballs are kicked once more. NSW declares itself to have beaten coronavirus.

And in early 2021, the vaccine arrives. We know it might not be a silver bullet, but everyone wants to believe that it is, and acts like it is. The jabs aren't arriving rapidly, or in large volumes, but we don't mind. We're happy to wait patiently while the virus stays at bay – and in Victoria. The southern state is a constant reminder that the threat of COVID is always looming, and perhaps a cue for governments and health departments to bolster their resources if the beast returns. But we seem to have made it through to the other side. Paramedics tear gowns off celebratorily, having survived a summer of being cooked sous vide in them. Only masks are compulsory for us now.

Then an unvaccinated limousine driver from Bondi sparks a chain of events that leads to the south-west doing what the south-west does best.

21
DELTA FARCE

The greatest myth about calling an ambulance is that it gets you dealt with faster at hospital. This couldn't be falser. If you happen to be in the throes of a genuine emergency, then yes, you will be seen without delay when we bring you in. No hospital is going to make you join the queue as you bleed to death from a stab wound or half your body stops working due to a stroke. But even so, if you self-present by a private vehicle or walk into an emergency department riddled with bullet holes or with a limb newly missing, you're not going to be sent to the waiting room while Mrs Wallis gets her eczema reviewed, either.

However, if like most of our callers, your chief complaint is something innocuous like tummy pain, a headache, sleeplessness or some lower back pain from a low-speed car park fender bender, you've only cost yourself more time by calling 000. If the acute section in the ED is full, the hospital cannot create beds out of thin air just because you've come in by ambulance. And leaving the hospital before being seen because the wait is too long when you've self-presented only to go home and call an ambulance to bring you back to get you seen quicker* won't just gift you with two very pissed-off paramedics, but is a direct ticket straight back to the end of the line.

If you call an ambulance, chances are you'll wait, sometimes hours depending on workload and the severity of your case, for us to arrive at your location. We'll then spend time at the scene, usually your house, assessing you. You will then be transported in a vehicle that has harboured unspeakable amounts of vomit, piss, shit, blood, decay and death, when you could have been chauffeured in luxury (or at least cleanliness) by a relative in your family sedan. You may not even be transported by us to the closest hospital or your preferred one – our destination is dictated by a computer algorithm that allocates a hospital based on its current capacity for ambulances and the nature of your medical problem.

On arrival at the hospital, you will then join the triage queue behind all the other ambulances that are lined up (sometimes as many as 15) and will be triaged with no great urgency because you are being minded by a pair of paramedics who have already assessed you, taken

* This happens disgustingly often.

your vital signs and concluded that you didn't need to be rushed to the resuscitation bay.

Once triaged, you will then be sent to the waiting room if you are young enough and healthy enough and capable of sitting on a chair*, where you will take your place at last on the list. Or, if you require a bed, you will remain on the ambulance stretcher until one becomes available and the other ambulances that arrived before you have offloaded their patients to beds first.

So, not only does this achieve nothing for you, but it also prevents us from responding to real emergencies for an unseen amount of time.

This has been the way since time immemorial.

Then the Delta variant arrives and makes this a thousand times worse.

We've known for well over a year that COVID could return at any time, coiled and ready to strike like a peckish cobra deciding on its next unsuspecting meal. But, in one of the greatest ever historical own goals, we celebrate too early. And we don't use the time to prepare. Well, our political leaders don't.

Coronavirus mutates into something deadlier and more transmissible, as every virus in the history of viruses has ever done. A vaccine has been developed and begun sauntering its way through healthcare workers

* Pretending you're not won't work.

and aged-care residents but is still unavailable to a large percentage of the public. And one of the vaccine brands has its reputation obliterated by internecine media reports, so nobody wants it, slowing things further. This only gives more ammunition to a coterie of intellectuals, such as football players' wives and essential oil enthusiasts, who have no intention of ever getting it anyway. So when the Delta variant wriggles its way out of a limousine in June 2021, we are far more vulnerable than we should have been. It's time to bust out the gowns again.

Staff morale plummets to an all-time low. Angus and I get dispatched to our fourth shortness-of-breath call of the day – which is what every call is for these days. But it doesn't prevent a frustrated groan and a swift smack of the steering wheel. We know the timewasters are going to keep coming, but every single one annoys us just as equally. Because there's only two ways the patient can present: super sick, in which case they'll be coughing and spluttering and breathing all over us while we're confined to the back of the ambulance with them, or hardly sick at all, in which case they won't need to go to hospital and have needlessly exposed us to this new COVID variant we know very little about.

Amir, a 25-year-old guy with no previous medical history and a very vocal anti-vaccine stance, has a sore throat and runny nose. We stare blankly. He stares back.

It's a medical Mexican standoff of disbelief. Us not believing he's called an ambulance for this. Him not believing we aren't rushing in and injecting him with a cure.

'So, you have COVID,' I say.

'Yes.'

'So . . . there's nothing we can do about that. There's no cure. It's a virus. You just have to wait it out until you get better. There was prevention, but you chose not to get that.'

'Too many people died from the vaccine.'

Four million people have died from COVID, you idiot.

'I think the risk of getting sick from COVID is much higher,' I say. 'I haven't been to anyone seriously ill who's had the vaccine. Everyone I've had to rush to hospital because of low oxygen levels wasn't vaccinated.'

'It's the communist government trying to control you. You're just another one of their sheep. You need to do more research before you go around telling people this stuff.'

In Russia, it's the legitimate communists who are screeching about COVID mandates like you clowns in Australia and the US.

'Sure, mate. Not sure why you've called us for help when you've already got all the answers,' I tell him.

'What should I do to get better?' Amir asks.

'Rest, drink water. And take Panadol for fevers. But you don't like taking medicine, so I guess that one's out of the question.'

'I think I need to go to hospital.'

'What for?'

'To be checked.'

'Checked for what? You know what's wrong. You have COVID. You've already done a test. So they don't even need to check that.'

'I think a doctor needs to check my lungs.'

Time for the spiel.

'Here's what's going to happen,' I begin. 'We'll drive you to hospital. Then you won't be allowed inside the hospital because there's no room, because it's full of people with COVID who wouldn't stay at home and get better. So you'll have to wait in the back of the ambulance. By yourself. Because I'm not sitting in there with you the whole time, because you have COVID. You could be in there for three, four, five hours. I have no idea. It all depends on when a space becomes free in the hospital. And that's not happening quickly because a) there's staff shortages because half of the staff are off sick with COVID and b) those staff who are left aren't in a rush to see healthy people in their 20s who have COVID and whose only problem is a runny nose and sore throat. You'll be sitting in the dark and the cold because we can't leave the ambulance running in the bay because it'll gas everyone with exhaust fumes. You won't be allowed out to use the bathroom, because you have COVID, so you can't use the waiting-room toilet. Then, eventually, when you make it inside, a doctor might listen to your lungs if he's feeling generous. Then he'll tell you to go home because you have COVID and there's nothing he can do about it and you shouldn't have come to hospital in the first place.

Then you'll wait a few more hours until a patient transport vehicle becomes available because you can't take public transport or a taxi home, because you have COVID. And if at any point during all of this you get sick of waiting and want to go home, you can't, because we don't drive people home because they're sick of waiting. We're an emergency service, not a taxi service. And, again, you can't use a taxi service. Because you have COVID.'

'I still think I should go.'

'Just get in the car,' I say, defeated.

'I think I might take some Panadol if you have any.'

'Sure, pal. You want the Pfizer or the AstraZeneca?'

We take Amir to Liverpool Hospital. And we wait. Hours and hours. Just like I told him we would. Then the nurse unit manager (NUM) approaches our ambulance. Amir's eyes light up. He thinks he's getting a bed. My eyes don't glow with the same enthusiasm, but I uncross my arms and shift my stance a little. I'm not excited, just relieved. Because my shift finished three hours ago and I haven't eaten since lunchtime, and by the time we finish sanitising the ambulance and getting back to the station and I drive home, it'll be at least 11pm until I get dinner. So I'm looking forward to that.

'Bad news, boys,' says Mary the NUM.

'The results are back for my headache and it's a haemorrhagic stroke?' asks Angus. 'No, wait, that would probably be a good thing at this point.'

'Nope, even better. The wards and ICU aren't moving and neither is the ED till tomorrow morning. Same for every other hospital that takes COVID patients between here and Royal North Shore. So that's where we're diverting you and every other COVID patient who gets brought in from now.'

'NORTH SHORE?' Amir and I say simultaneously.

I angrily rip off my PPE so I can retrieve my phone that's stuck in a pocket under my gown and text my partner. I tell her not to stay up and wait for me to come home for dinner. I won't be home until tomorrow now. Even though I was supposed to finish my day shift three hours ago. Then I put all my PPE back on for the drive north. My phone buzzes a few minutes into the journey. I'll have to check what it says in an hour, if I'm not unconscious from low blood sugar. But at least I'll be in an ambulance.

There weren't many funny stories coming out of this period. It was difficult to see the humour in the petty calls because they weren't just so interminable, they were also incredibly risky to us personally. The nights, as always, were the biggest battle. Fewer staff were rostered, and when you factor in those isolating and those who decided to use up some sick leave because they'd just had enough, it often meant a ratio of just one or two ambulances for every 100,000 people in the area. Knowing there's no more help out there to combat the endless calls made it hard to care anymore, even though caring is what we signed up to do. And who knew if our vaccine was starting to wear off.

They call it compassion fatigue, when you work around trauma and illness so frequently it exhausts you to the point where you start losing the ability to empathise. I think it's more to do with the fact that we are expected to do the most humane job in the world but have the inhuman ability to be completely non-judgemental towards people who have no regard for anyone but themselves. Any ambo who argues otherwise probably owns one of those cringey paintings of a paramedic where there's an angelic ghost hovering above, resting a spectral hand on their shoulder as they cry while trying to save someone who's beyond help.

We gown up; we transport; we clean. Gown up, transport, clean. Gown up, leave patient at home, clean. Gown up, transport, clean. Rinse and repeat. There's no rushing to get the car ready between jobs anymore. Another shortness-of-breath call won't tug at the heartstrings like it used to. The dispatchers can plead all they want, but when you work hard, you are immediately rewarded with more work as soon as you are done with your current task. So instead of being over-enthusiastic, it's better to just take your time. The salary stays the same.

As much as we hate wearing PPE, it's essential – and the one thing that's improved from the last wave. There's no shortage of masks because there's been plenty of time to manufacture them. We actually have enough PPE now. And we need it. Every case is COVID. Or if it's not, we still treat it like it is. Because Fairfield is the epicentre at this moment. Households of ten or more are ravaged with the spicy cough and we are flung into the middle of them all. Some houses are completely symptomatic, the residents infecting every surface they touch but only wanting one person to be 'checked'. Some are symptomatic but haven't been tested because they're still unaware of the virus that's been circulating for the past 18 months and has broken the world. Some have been tested but insist '*it's not COVID*', despite a positive test confirming otherwise.

'*The hospital doesn't know what they're talking about*,' they say.

Nothing is surprising; everything is infuriating.

Angus and I rush to help a crew that's called IC backup for a patient who's gone into cardiac arrest on them. It's an elderly female, self-isolating with her daughter-in-law in her apartment because they've tested positive when the rest of the family hasn't. It's an awkward situation about to be made a whole lot more awkward.

We walk in on two female paramedics taking turns pumping furiously on the woman's chest. We have no idea who they are; faces are unrecognisable under goggles and P2 masks, and name badges and rank epaulettes are obscured by gowns.

The girls breathlessly introduce themselves and the senior officer gives me a patient handover. The lady was in hospital this morning with shortness of breath, then self-discharged against advice. She isn't vaccinated. She's elderly and has extensive medical history. She called an ambulance again tonight with severe breathing difficulties. Within minutes, she had no difficulty breathing – because she stopped completely. She rolled the dice by not getting the vaccine, against all medical advice, and has now thrown up snake eyes.

The monitor shows a flatline, and 17 minutes on the timer. Twenty minutes of no response is when we give up. I don't pull out the LUCAS device. Her frail ribcage has already been ground into powdery dust by the compressions. I don't intubate the woman. We know this is futile. We're only going to be aerosolising more COVID spores for no reason. Nobody can gain intravenous access to her shrivelled veins. I don't pull out the EZ-IO drill. At the absolute best, this would allow us to give her a shot of adrenaline that might achieve a feeble heartbeat, which wouldn't last long before disappearing again. We'd just be prolonging the inevitable.

We stop CPR and cease all resuscitation. We tell the daughter-in-law the news.

'What happens now?' she asks.

Shock and confusion are hitting her more than grief right now.

'Well, the police will have to come. You're not in trouble; it's just a formality every time there's an unexpected death in a home. They won't be too long, though. The hospital paperwork here has her diagnosis and her medical history,' I say, holding up the discharge letter. 'So there's not much they need to investigate.'

'Then you guys take her away, right?'

'No, sorry, that's not what we do. A funeral home will have to do that.'

The realisation is starting to hit her. She must call her partner and tell him his mother has just died. Then she must spend the rest of the night in this apartment, alone with the body, until a funeral director can come in the morning and take it away, unable to offer much sympathy or compassion under the cold, clinical garb of PPE that's normal for them now too.

There was time to mitigate this. Nearly 18 months passed between COVID first entering the country and the Delta wave. Those in power had the means and the money to better prepare us. But instead of bolstering healthcare workers, they clapped us and said 'thanks' for a week back in March 2020 and then, as always, left us to figure it out with the limited resources we had. Because the system is coping. No matter how bad things get, the system always copes. That's what the public keeps being told, anyway. It's a miracle there even is a system anymore. Because if healthcare wasn't now fortified as the most secure job industry in existence, thanks to what COVID has shown us, staff would be looking elsewhere. People don't quit jobs; they quit the people they work for. Everyone in healthcare pulled together and got through the worst of Delta in spite of the decisions being made at the top. Not because of them. And for us paramedics on the coalface, it was no surprise, considering the public ignorance and malicious non-compliance we witnessed every day. They played a part in electing these officials.

The American comedian George Carlin warned us about this before he died: if you have selfish, ignorant citizens, you're going to get selfish, ignorant leaders.

Someone should have listened.

22

KICKSTART MY HEART

A familiar face and oversized body I haven't seen in years lumbers towards the ambulance I'm checking over. My regular partner texted earlier in the day to say he wasn't coming in tonight. Sick leave is being used by everyone with increasing regularity these days, particularly for night shifts. So I've come in early to make sure the car is up to scratch in case I'm working solo.

Big Phil starts cheerfully singing the opening words to 'Reunited' by Peaches & Herb as he dumps his kit bag in front of me.

'What the hell are you singing, mate?' I say as we shake hands and exchange a hug.

It's been six years since we last worked a shift together, but immediately I can tell Phil's aged more than 20 in that time. A divorce, a thousand triple cheeseburgers and the general toll of being a paramedic in south-west

Sydney during the pandemic hasn't been kind to him. His eyes are sunken into his skull and the tissue underneath is dark and puffy from six more years of shift-work sleep deprivation. His bulk is far softer than the brawn it once was. His eyes, cheeks and nose remain a constantly flushed red, and the cigarette stains on his fingers are set in deeper than ever before. His hair has thinned to wisps and the wraith-like pallor of his skin is whiter than the edge of Stevie Nicks' credit card.

'I'm on an overtime shift, buddy. It's you and me working together again!' he says.

'On the dollars. Nice, mate. You got an anniversary present to pay for or something?'

'Nah, sadly nothing that exciting. Been doing a few more shifts here and there for some extra cash to help Mum out. She's still struggling after she had COVID a few months ago and the respiratory specialist appointments aren't cheap. Not for a pensioner anyway. And you want to know the silliest thing . . . you've got to walk up 10 stairs to get to his office. Poor Mum can barely do that!'

'Shit, that's rough. Tell you what, you drive tonight. Let's have an easy, fun night like the old days.'

'Aw thanks, mate. We can swap over halfway if you want. Doesn't really matter though, you're the big, fancy intensive care paramedic in the flash intensive care car now, so you're doing all the work anyway.'

'Ha, I wish that were the case. It's that busy that we pick up the minor COVIDs and constipations just like everyone else these days.'

'Yeah, I thought moving further south of Macquarie Fields was my ticket out of the chaos, but it's the same everywhere. I'm well past trying to get into the ICP course now, so I don't know what the secret is to lasting in this job anymore. Anyway, let's go get some food and coffee before it all kicks off.'

Phil cruises past the hospital on the way to find somewhere that will sell us takeaway coffees at 7pm that isn't a McDonald's. We see the day shift crews lined up in the ambulance bay, still waiting to offload their patients. There's a random RAV4 pulled into one of the spots and we see one of our colleagues giving the driver a spray, yelling at him that the parking space is for ambulances only and that he needs to move in case an emergency comes in. It's a scene I'd usually find amusing but coupled with Phil's musings on being too far gone to become an ICP, and the way he's looking right now, it gets me thinking about how tiring all this is becoming and the toll it's taking on me as well.

Phil's career prospects and aspirations lie dead in the water of his past. He's just grinding for a stable income now. Not even working to live anymore. Working to *survive*. He's another dehydrated cell in the increasingly anaemic bloodstream of an attenuated workforce. It's like gazing into a crystal ball. But unlike Phil, I'm at a crossroads. It feels like I'm at the stage of my career that's mirroring where Phil was when he trained me. I still have options. But after those six short years, Phil reminds me of how old and burnt out Terry was when I first worked with him.

I've got a few choices to spark the catalyst for change, but none are without caveats. I could forgo the relationships I've forged and the modern conveniences that city life offers and opt for a quieter rural posting in regional Australia. Or I could move into the white-collar ranks of ambulance personnel who work behind desks and get better pay packets without the dangers of being at the coalface and the punishment of night shifts. But I worked a desk job before this, and the extra days off and not staying in the same place throughout the workday is what appealed to me in the first place. Plus, the culture of stultifying managerialism that's displaced conventional leadership in our industry is another deterrent from taking that path. It would be like abandoning the diggers to become an officer, leaving the proletariat in favour of the bourgeoisie. It's got all the noble intentions of effecting change one has when entering politics, but just like politics, the corporate management of this industry destroys one's integrity towards those who work below them. *I'd rather not get involved in any of that*, I think to myself.

'Who's paying?'

Phil's question snaps me out of my trance. Suddenly we're standing across from a cash register where we've just ordered two long blacks. I don't even remember walking into the place.

'Err . . . you! You're the one making double-time tonight, ya stingy bastard,' I reply.

'When you've picked up your cappuccinos, I've got a breathing problem for you in Miller.'

The ever-ominous voice of the dispatcher, who's obviously tracking our current location on his map, doles out our first case for the night.

'Breathing problems. Why don't they just say outright that it's a bloody COVID job?' grunts Phil as we walk back to the ambulance.

Without any irony, he takes a drag from an electronic vape before climbing into the driver's seat. *Good to see he's made progress from the Winnie Reds*, I think to myself.

The job notes on the data terminal confirm that the patient has COVID. By now we know to expect it, but nonetheless it still annoys us a little every time. On the way to the job, Phil tells me he's considering becoming a vegan after watching a Netflix documentary that showed the change in diet could slow the effects of heart disease – a silent killer of regular people but a mass murderer of shift workers. Seems like the vape isn't the only small change he's making. I silently hope he does do something because he's not looking too great. Mates like him are one of the few good things we have left in this job.

We head inside a typical fibro house in Miller, and a strange sense of déjà vu comes over me. This isn't an uncommon phenomenon in the ambulance world, as we often return to the scenes of former crimes, some far too often, and patients start to recognise us, even get to know us a little more personally than we're sometimes comfortable with. But I don't remember ever attending this address.

'Hang on, weren't you the bloke that was at the hospital before?' Phil says to the man who opens the door.

It hits me. The RAV4 parked in the driveway.

'Yes, yes. That was me. But there was no parking. So I drove home and called. It's for my wife. She's in here. She can't breathe.'

We enter a living room and see a middle-aged woman on a couch. Texting on her phone. No distress. No change in colour. No gasping for air. Not an emergency in sight.

'iPhone positive,' I whisper to Phil, using a term I'm fairly sure he taught me.

'Wait . . . so you drove to the hospital because you reckon your wife can't breathe, and because you couldn't find a park you turned around and drove home and called 000?' Phil asks the man.

A flash of scarlet is beginning to fill his chalky face.

'Yes, we didn't know what to do so we came home and called the ambulance.'

'Didn't know what to do . . . stop out the front and take her inside the bloody . . . ahh never mind.'

Phil no longer has the energy to be a one-man David against society's Goliath of stupidity. The redness in his face fades and the calm, composed Phil who initiated me into this crazy world of paramedicine returns.

'Alright love, when did you start feeling short of breath?' he asks.

'As soon as she took the RAT test and it came up positive,' says the husband answering for her.

Phil sighs.

'Okay, look there's no need to worry. You're absolutely fine. You don't suddenly die of COVID the second you test positive on a RAT. Just like you don't get chest pain the second the vaccine needle goes into your arm. That's called anxiety.'

'Oh, she's not vaccinated.'

Phil's patience is being properly tested now. But he remains the constant professional and lists the signs and symptoms the lady and her husband need to watch out for and when it's appropriate to call an ambulance or go to hospital. He even looks up on his phone if there's any nearby chemists with Sp02 monitors in stock. We leave the lady to recover at home. As we exit the house, the husband spies some writing on the side of our vehicle.

'Oh, I didn't know we were getting an emergency ambulance; we only wanted a regular ambulance for a check-up.'

Phil looks like he's about to say something but just shakes his head and keeps walking. I can't help myself: 'No such thing as a regular ambulance, pal. They're all supposed to be for emergencies.'

'Dinner time,' says Phil.

He starts driving while I complete our non-transport paperwork in the passenger seat. We eventually come to a stop and when I look up, we're in the car park of the McDonald's on Hoxton Park Road.

'What happened to becoming vegan?' I ask.

'They sell salads here.'

Sure enough, Phil returns to the car with two plastic boxes full of lettuce and tomato, and for the first time in my life, I eat a salad from Macca's. And now that we're in the safety of the car, and with a gutful of food, Phil's ranting begins.

'I can't believe selfish, ignorant, unvaccinated clowns like that! Those sorts of morons are the whole reason Mum can't walk upstairs anymore, and I've got to do all these bloody extra shifts just to get by. And now they're talking about letting that Novak Djokovic dickhead play in the Australian Open. What hope do we have when pricks like him are worshipped as celebrities? Just gives all these imbeciles more self-righteousness. That bloke may as well change his name to *No-vax* Djokovic.'

A blazing cinnabar colour has completely covered Phil's face now. I can't resist stirring the pot a little.

'He's a vegan, you know.'

'Oh what? For fuck's sa–'

He stops speaking and for a second, I think he's choked on a crouton. *Lucky he's with me and I'm experienced with chokings*, I think.

'What's wrong n–'

I look up from my bowl and turn to face him. Now it's me that can't speak. I drop my plastic fork into the footwell.

'Shit, you alright, mate?' I ask.

'Yep, yep, I'm fine,' he gasps.

He's not. His skin has changed colour again and now it's ashen grey. Beads of sweat slide down his temples and hit his collar like raindrops. I instantly know what's wrong.

'Fuck, get out of that seat and get on the bloody stretcher,' I say.

'Nah mate, I'm alright, I'm alright. I'll just drive us down the road and get checked out at the hospital.'

'You're not bloody driving me anywhere like this! Now get out and get on the fucking stretcher!'

I'm getting impatient because I know his stubbornness is going to be his undoing, just as I've seen happen to hundreds of patients. When I finish yelling at him, Phil winces as a pang of sharp pain hits him in the chest. He brings a hand up to his sternum, clutching the area.

'Alright, alright, I'll get on the bloody stretcher.'

'How long's this been going on for?' I ask in a motherly tone as he lays down on the gurney.

'Ahh, just a few days,' he groans.

'A FEW DAYS! And you have the gall to lecture patients on putting off their health issues while you've been walking around with chest pains for a few days. Now take off your bloody shirt so I can do an ECG.'

'Alright, calm down.'

This feels weird. I've never treated a colleague before, let alone the bloke who taught me how to be a paramedic. And I don't even need to do Phil's ECG, because I know exactly what it's going to show. But just in case I'm overreacting, and have been blinded by panic, I want to make sure. And I don't want to look stupid when I wheel him through the doors of the ED, either.

'Of course you're a hairy bastard,' I say, looking at Phil's chest when he removes the top half of his uniform.

I fish out one of the cheap disposable razors we use to shave patients' body hair so that our ECG electrodes stick to their skin and begin shearing. My hands are trembling.

'Hurry up, Muhammad Ali,' he says.

I'm glad he's taking this as seriously as I am. I've been an ICP long enough now that there's very little which unsettles me. I've treated toddlers in cardiac arrest, motorcyclists missing limbs and palliative care patients surrounded by their entire family as they take their last breath. But this is different. Way different.

The ECG monitor beeps and spits out a small rectangle of pink paper covered in squiggly lines. They're not the squiggly lines I want to see. They're the bad kind. And they're not even the lesser of the bad kind of squiggly lines that an ECG can produce. They're an array of little black tombstone shapes that signify an occlusion of Phil's left anterior descending artery. This artery is called The Widowmaker for a reason. Of all the types of heart attacks, this one is the worst.

'Alright stay there and don't move. Let's get you to the hospital,' I say.

'It's bad, isn't it?'

'Could be worse. You could be working with Terry.'

There isn't a lot that forces me to drive like Paulini anymore, that novelty has long since worn off. But if ever a time has called for an unbridled blast to the resus bay, it's now. I haven't got time to mess around transmitting Phil's

ECG to a cardiologist or be sticking a cannula in him. I'm by myself and there's no one else around to help. From listening to the radio, I know that everyone else is either on a job or stuck in bed block at the hospital. Phil could go into cardiac arrest at any moment; the best thing to do for him right now is get him onto a hospital bed ASAP.

Over the radio, I ask the dispatcher to call the hospital's 'bat phone' and tell them I'm bringing in a 45-year-old male having a STEMI*, and that they'll need to open the cardiac cath lab.

'They're asking for you to transmit an ECG before they open the cath lab,' replies the dispatcher after about 30 seconds of silence.

'There's no bloody time for that! Just tell them to trust me!' I yell into the radio.

We're crossing the Hume Highway, only a few minutes from the hospital when Phil calls out.

'Mate, I'm not feeling too good back here.'

I hear the beeping of the heart monitor slow to a rate that's well below normal. Then Phil has a huge, projectile chunder. Things just got a whole lot worse.

'Mate, you better not bloody die back there. No way I'm doing that paperwork. If you're gonna croak, do it in the hospital. And use a bloody vomit bag would you, otherwise you're cleaning, too.'

Dark times call for dark humour.

---

* ST-elevation myocardial infarction – the technical name for a bad heart attack. Not that there's such thing as a 'good' heart attack, but some are worse than others.

'If I do cark it,' Phil replies. 'Just tell them it happened as soon as you started pulling the stretcher out. That's technically not in the ambulance, right?'

Phil's wiping vomit from his lips as a surge of life jolts back into him. I always tell patients that sometimes all you need is a good spew to feel better. It's just the burst he needs to see all the shocked and worried faces of our colleagues crowding around as I reverse into the ambulance bay. My panicked tone on the radio was obviously heard by someone and the word has gotten round that something very unusual is coming into the resus area. There's a team of doctors and nurses huddled at the doors as well.

'How is he?' a senior staff specialist asks me as I pull the stretcher out the back of the ambulance.

I hand the ECG printout to the doctor without saying a word.

'Straight up to the cath lab,' he says. 'They're waiting for you.'

Everyone wants to help, but there's nothing they can offer. Phil needs someone who can sort out the chunk of atherosclerotic plaque that's blocking blood flow to the most important chamber of his heart, and not even the most skilled paramedic can do that. The ambos stay behind while the staff specialist and two nurses accompany me with emergency resus gear while I push the stretcher into the lift. The ECG monitor continues to beep at an increasingly sluggish rate. Phil hasn't said anything in a while.

'Long shot, but you wouldn't happen to know when he last ate, by any chance?' the anaesthetist asks me.

'Actually, I do,' I reply. 'It was a McDonald's salad. About 10 minutes ago.'

'Bugger. Oh well, he needs to be put under. I'll just do my best and hope he doesn't aspirate*.'

From behind the glass screen of a viewing room, I watch the anaesthetist knock Phil out with a cocktail of sedatives and paralytic drugs as he lays under a sheet on the operating table in the crowded cath lab.

'Just a bit of champagne to get you off to sleep,' he says as he pushes the IV medications into Phil's lifeless body.

That's largely why he's ended up here, I think.

Then I observe the same anaesthetist struggle to intubate Phil. I sympathise, having had to perform the same procedure myself on patients with elevated BMIs.

Making things difficult for everyone to the end, you fat bastard.

I know Phil would appreciate the rib. After what seems like minutes of apnoea, but is probably more like 30 seconds, the anaesthetist slides the breathing tube into Phil's oversized trachea and places him onto a ventilator. He's been successfully anaesthetised. Now it's time for the cardiologist to earn his coin.

He gains access into Phil's femoral artery and inserts a wire that runs from his upper leg all the way to his heart so that the blockage can be rectified. Foggy shapes

---

* Vomit into your lungs during anaesthesia. This is why you're made to fast before elective surgery.

move around on ultrasonic screens set up around the room while the procedure takes place. I have no idea what any of them mean. Everyone seems a bit too busy for me to ask how things are going. Then alarms start going off. Voices get raised and physicians and nurses start doing things hurriedly. A pair of defibrillator pads get placed on Phil's chest. This is the only time in my life I've wished I had more medical ignorance.

Then the alarms stop.

Fuck, he's dead. No one's moving. WHY ISN'T ANYBODY MOVING?

I'm about to bang on the glass and turn my thoughts into very loud, very angry words, when the cardiologist looks up. He gives me a thumbs up.

'What just happened?' I say to the radiographer sitting at a desk next to me, looking at a bank of black-and-white screens full of medical imagery.

'Look,' he says pointing to one of the monitors.

I can't even read the basics of an X-ray, but even my novice mind can tell what's going on. Little winding lines all over the screen are suddenly turning from faded grey to solid black. They're like little estuaries flooding with water after a great dam has been opened. But it's not water. It's blood. Glorious, oxygenated, nutrient-filled, life-giving blood. And the little estuaries are the vessels of Phil's left ventricle that, as of a few seconds ago, were completely blocked and about to kill him.

'The stent went in nicely,' the cardiologist tells me. 'But that was one of the nastiest Widowmakers I've seen in a long time, so we're going to keep him under for a while before we wake him up. It was a pretty hard ordeal on his heart, but he'll be alright. He'll need to give up the smokes and change his diet, though. There'll be a few daily medications in his routine now as well.'

'Ha, I'll let him know when he wakes up. Thanks, Doc.'

I stay by Phil's side all night, watching him – with the assistance of Propofol and Fentanyl – have the most peaceful sleep he'll ever experience. I think about how long it's been and how nice it would be to get some shut-eye like that.

'Time to go home, sleepy.'

I jolt awake. A hand is squeezing my shoulder.

'Mate, get the hell out of here,' says Chad. 'Go home and get some rest. Phil's going to be alright. They've decided to keep him under for the rest of today as well, so you're not achieving anything just sitting here. Plus, work doesn't want to pay you overtime rates to sit on your arse.'

'What time is it?' I mumble, looking down at my watch. 'Oh.'

'Yep.'

It's 6.45am. The shift is almost over. And Chad's right; work doesn't like paying overtime rates at the best of times, let alone when I'm not doing anything to earn them.

'I'll stay here with Phil,' he says. 'Just get out of here.'

I mosey back to the station in the ambulance, one crew member fewer than what I started the shift with. When I pull in, there's no one around. Day shift are already out on jobs; night shift still stuck at the hospital. I want to grab a beer from the station's beer fridge, just like Big Phil did all those years ago at the end of my first night shift when he was training me. Back when I was repulsed by the thought of an ice-cold stubby at quarter to seven in the morning. But it wasn't long after that night that beer fridges were taken from us too, the reason rumoured to be because a student paramedic got pissed after a shift and copped a DUI on the way home. So it was no more beers for anyone. Nowadays, alcohol-inspired decompression and team bonding has been replaced with online mindfulness courses and wellness apps. The cruel joke is that the underlying message is always about being less stressed and getting more sleep.

I settle for a cup of instant Moccona and start thinking about all the things I'm going to do with my five days off.

EPILOGUE

I don't work in south-west Sydney anymore. After six long years I've moved far away, swapping the chaos of metropolitan ambulance work for the hope of a more relaxed country lifestyle. I've succeeded in 'buying the farm', as wartime blokes used to dream about (but usually ended up dying on the fields of a farm somewhere overseas instead). The people who inspired Chad, Mark, Danielle, Rhiannon and Angus have all moved on, too, whether it be into different specialties or different locations. But the Phils, Wendys and Terrys of our little ambulance bubble will never leave the area, at least not until they retire. They're from a different generation, where impulsive career and lifestyle changes don't happen on a whim as often as they do with us younger lot. They're institutions, in a way. And their length of service is not just impressive; it's incomparable – likely to never be repeated by the new breed of paramedic. The average lifespan of an ambo nowadays is thought to be less than five years. I've already bested that, working in the busiest, most challenging area of NSW. But my relatively short time is nothing compared to the multiple lifetimes lived by legends like Phil, Wendy and Terry. I just hope the destruction wreaked upon the healthcare industry by COVID-19 eventually creates cause for change so that the next generation of paramedics have it better than they (and to a much lesser extent, I) did.

The south-west didn't say goodbye to me without a parting gift. Just like when I copped a gastro bug from a patient after my first ever shift, I started feeling off in the days following my final one in Liverpool, too. Remembering the teeming numbers of mosquitoes swarming outside Liverpool Hospital in the early morning hours at the end of the shift, I thought to myself: *This is it! Japanese encephalitis or monkeypox has got me! This is how it ends!*

I did the responsible thing and took a RAT test. The two pink lines confirmed my fears to be unfounded. My headache wasn't brain inflammation, and the mild fever wasn't from monkeypox. More than two years since it first arrived in the country, and after attending hundreds of patients with varying degrees of severity, and myself having varying degrees of protection via vaccination or PPE, I had finally caught COVID-19. I'd been living under the illusion that I was born with a superbloodline that made me immune. But alas, I'm not special.

Just like everyone else, I'm susceptible to the wrath of this world-breaking virus.

I remember the patient who I'm convinced gave it to me. It was the last job of the day, an older lady who was extremely unwell at the best of times. She'd had a double-lung transplant earlier in life and was also in end-stage renal failure, meaning she had to attend dialysis three times a week. How she had made it to a sixth day of being COVID-positive was a miracle in itself but today was the first time she'd felt the need to call an ambulance after feeling short of breath. On further examination, it turned out she'd been feeling breathless since walking back to her car from her dialysis appointment earlier in the morning. She'd managed to drive home, and it was now early in the evening. She was feeling fine by the time we arrived, and her vitals all checked out okay. Her GP had even agreed to see her earlier in the week (another miracle) and had prescribed her a new antiviral medication, so she was being actively treated. She told us that the earlier episode was probably just her anxiety playing up, but that she'd feel safer going to hospital in case it happened again. When I asked her why she waited hours to call, she said she thought ambulances weren't available at night, so she'd better get one in before we shut up shop for the day.

Despite her appearing fine outwardly, and my conclusion that, yes, the episode was likely just anxiety, I couldn't recommend that she stay at home given her risk factors; the two most obvious ones being the fleshy lobes in her chest responsible for her breathing that weren't even her own. The final kicker was she wanted to be transported to the hospital where her dialysis took place, meaning we'd be bypassing three closer ones (*'That's where they've got all my records!'* she said). Usually this isn't a request we have to abide by. After all, in an emergency, a patient should get to the closest hospital as quickly as possible. We wouldn't drive someone to a hospital on the Gold Coast because that's where all their records are if they happened to be holidaying in Sydney at the time. But on the final job of my final shift in Sydney, I was feeling generous and was happy to entertain the use of our services for convenience one last time – especially for a nice old bird.

The moment I knew I'd stuffed up was when, during the drive to the hospital, she began pulling her mask down to cough and complaining that wearing it made her feel anxious. This would have only lasted five minutes had we transported her to the closest hospital, but thanks to my altruism and the peak-hour traffic, I was stuck in the germ incubator that is the back of an ambulance with a COVID-positive patient for 45 minutes. No good deed ever goes unpunished.

At the time of writing, there have been a plethora of strains and sub-strains of COVID-19. There's no end in sight for when the coronavirus might go away. New variants continue to be reported overseas every few months and rapidly seep their way into Australia. Scores of patients continue to call ambulances every day, some starving of oxygen as their lungs disintegrate from the disease, but most with very mild symptoms and the accompanying paranoia that a minor cough or sore throat is about to kill them.

More paramedics are on the way is the promise we keep hearing from the powers-that-be above. But does throwing greater numbers at the problem of trivial calls and minor maladies fix it? Or does it create a greater swell in an ever-diluting sea of highly trained paramedics, a swell that aims to collect all the flotsam of non-emergencies, while only leading to a widespread de-skilling of the workforce when the treasure of attending a real emergency becomes ever rarer.

And will us healthcare workers be wearing masks forever? Are there going to be vaccine-resistant variants of COVID-19? How many more vaccines and booster shots are there going to be? Will an extremely mild variant take over and render coronavirus no worse than the common cold? Or will an entirely new disease emerge and cause another pandemic? Will we have learned enough lessons from this one?

No paramedic, nurse, doctor or even scientist has the answer. The only people who claim to know everything are the mums of Facebook with too much time on their hands and the conspiracy theorists of Reddit and encrypted messaging apps. And while for any reasonable person these answers are clearly not the right ones, they keep us healthcare workers snug in our job security – as tired and frustrated as the profession continues to make us.

Rarely do I ever tell a stranger the truth when they ask what I do for work. Not because I'm ashamed or anything, but because I know the next question they're going to follow up with. Instead, I come up with all sorts of creative job descriptors: pest management, Uber driver, natural selection interventionist. Now I have one more vocation to add: writer. This answer will be true, at least, but I still won't be able to avoid the question.

'What do you write about?' they'll ask.

If I want to sell this book, I'll have to answer truthfully: 'Being a paramedic.'

And here it comes. *Cue cringe.*

'A paramedic? You must've seen some terrible things!'

It's the obvious statement to make. But now they're expecting a live-action, grisly retelling of the sorts of maiming and dismemberment that make true-crime podcasts so successful.

'Not as often as you think,' I'll reply.

'Oh really? Why not?'

'You'll have to read the book,' I'll say.

Because hopefully, what this book shows is that being an ambo is much more than blood and guts. All the stories recounted in this book are from a microcosm. They're from one paramedic working in a specific area for a specific organisation at specific times. They're a tiny drop of fluid sitting at the tip of a gigantic syringe when it comes to the wild tales of being a paramedic and working in healthcare in general. They're a microscopic slice from all the forgotten calls of the past, and the infinite number of calls to come in the future that, as long paramedics continue to service the public, will have them thinking to themselves at least once every day: '*You called an ambulance* for what?'

AUTHOR'S NOTE

The events that take place in this book are all true. All except the last story about Big Phil's heart attack. While I have had the unfortunate honour of treating a fellow paramedic in my career, this particular story is a minor embellishment that's intended to represent the far-too-numerous colleagues who've suffered life-altering medical or mental health issues that this job no doubt played either a small or large part in. Whether it be crippling back injuries, medical retirement from long COVID symptoms or saddest of all, death from the likes of heart disease and suicide, the story of Big Phil is a cautionary tale about a lucky escape. Sadly, not all have been able to avoid the damage dealt by occupational stress, and this has been one of my main motivations for writing this book: to challenge the public to think twice before calling 000, because every trivial call adds to a toll on another human being who only wants to help those genuinely in need.

For the rest of the stories, I lived them and have reproduced them here as faithfully as possible, without embellishment, based on memory and notes I took at the time. I can guarantee you that after each story recounted here, the phrase 'You can't make this shit up,' or 'Only in the south-west,' was uttered by either myself or a colleague – or at least the thought crossed our minds.

To protect their privacy, the names, ages and locations of patients have, however, been altered, as have the names, ages and personalities of my colleagues. The fictional identities I have created for my work partners are a merging of personalities drawn from the hundreds of people I have worked with, and certainly not based on any individual person. The dialogue is also real and has been recounted as accurately as I can remember.

The order of events in this book has also been compressed and altered for narrative purposes, but this has not affected the individual stories themselves. For obvious reasons, it would be impossible to recount every moment of every job in my career. It would also be extremely boring in a lot of places, so while every case occurred at some point in my career, not every case occurred at the time it does in the book, or with the partner who was with me.

There is much dark humour and foul language in this book as well. This is the reality of being a paramedic. It isn't all rainbows and unicorns, and it certainly isn't a carefully curated reality TV show that's been heavily edited for an organisation to preserve a certain image. Without a heavy smattering of gallows humour and some words or thoughts ambulance services would rather you didn't read, it just wouldn't be a genuine recount of a paramedic's journey.

The views and attitudes expressed in this book are mine and mine alone, and do not necessarily reflect those of my employer or my colleagues. And more importantly, they should also not discourage you from calling for an ambulance in the case of a genuine emergency.

ACKNOWLEDGEMENTS

Firstly, I would like to thank Lewis Isaacs, whose opinion I always hold in the highest regard. Without the positive feedback you provided on my early written anecdotes, I would never have continued with this project beyond a couple of draft chapters.

To Vince Jackson, a colleague from my former career and the only person I wanted to proofread my words and knock them into shape when the time came to submit them to publishers. Your sharp eye, limitless knowledge and understanding of my sense of humour got this project over the line. And to the rest of the fellas from the *Top Gear* days, whose genius writing was the best in the country at the time, you all inspired my style and humour and I will forever sit at your feet when it comes to the written word.

To my current colleagues (if I'm still employed as a paramedic after this book comes out), particularly all of those that worked with me in the south-west, hopefully this message gets absorbed by at least a few members of the public and buys you a little bit of downtime on shift. Change needs to come from many different parties, though, and I hope my story can contribute to it in a positive way, not just for us ambos, but also for ED nurses, doctors, fireys, cops and other frontline workers as well – we've all had a rough go of it lately. Even when we build a thousand bridges, they never call us bridge builders.

Also, to my real training officers (both during my probation and ICP training), who are all very different from the fictional identities in this book, thank you for the foundations you gave me. You pushed and challenged me, and the successes I've had are in large part due to your commitment. It certainly wasn't as easy as the book makes out to meet your standards (particularly ICP!) and I hope you all get a laugh from the monster you helped create.

To any lawyers and union representatives whose assistance I may require in the future, thanks in advance.

To Alex Lloyd, Belinda Huang, Sam Sainsbury and the rest of the team (especially legal) from Pan Macmillan that worked with me on this project – your enthusiasm and support for my vision of turning some silly work stories into a serious message for everyone to read has been such an unexpected gift, and I am forever grateful for it.

And lastly, to Fiona and Bear, who are the best things in the world to come home to after a long day (or night) at work.